Introduction to Beauty

Introduction

to

BEAUTY

By

Van Meter Ames

Essay Index Reprint Series

BOOKS FOR LIBRARIES PRESS, INC.
FREEPORT, NEW YORK

BH
201
.A5
1968
153240
May 1991

To My Father
EDWARD SCRIBNER AMES
PHILOSOPHER AND MINISTER

CONTENTS

Acknowledgments

MY WIFE has given me the most valuable help with the plan of the book as a whole, with the organization of each chapter, and with the structure of many sentences. Mr. William T. Bissell, of Harper & Brothers, has given very helpful advice about the manuscript, and I am very grateful to several friends who have read parts of it and made suggestions. It is not the fault of Mr. Henry Woodward, young Cincinnati composer, or of Professor Ralph M. Blake of Brown University, that the chapter on music is not a better one. My friend, Mr. G. G. Dodds of New York City, connoisseur of fine bookmaking, gave me the idea of including a chapter on printing.

The substance of the second chapter appeared under the title of "Æsthetic Experience" in *Essays in Philosophy*, edited by T. V. Smith and W. K. Wright, The Open Court Publishing Co., 1929.

Acknowledgments

The twelfth chapter appeared in somewhat different form as an article called "Business and Art" in *The International Journal of Ethics*, Vol. XLI, No. 1, October, 1930.

V. M. A.

Preface

FORMERLY there was assumed to be a special faculty, called taste, with which beauty was appreciated; and a strange power, called genius, with which beauty was created. Lately it has been maintained that there are only certain objects, or only some aspects of objects, the formal aspects, in which beauty may be discerned; and that only the satisfaction of the desire for abstract form can be æsthetic satisfaction. Finally, there is still a wide belief that works of art are very different from the other works of man. But the thesis of this book is that the whole man, the entire psycho-physical organism, is involved in æsthetic experience; that anything in the world which satisfies any desire may be regarded as beautiful; that anyone who uses intelligence and skill to fill a need is an artist; and that every work of man which ministers to want is a work of art.

It seems to the author that art and beauty have no understandable meaning unless their value can be explained in terms of their usefulness in satisfying needs. The difficulty with this explanation is that it draws no line between art and the rest of life. The author confesses that he does not know how to draw such a line without doing it arbitrarily and unfairly. To him any life, and any part of life, in which needs are skillfully satisfied, is fine art.

PART ONE

ÆSTHETIC THEORY

Chapter One

THE NATURE OF BEAUTY

THE path to beauty is what we are all trying to find and to follow. To define beauty as that which is sought, as it appears in imagination, is sufficient to show that everyone is seeking beauty, for it cannot be denied that everyone is looking for something and dreaming about it. To dispute taste is futile, because beauty varies for different people and for the same person. The vulgar have their beauty, the lofty theirs. But the vulgar have moments in which they may appreciate another beauty, and so have the lofty.

Beauty is not entirely a personal affair, because the most subjective things are an objective part of human nature which is universal; as the hidden arrangements in one house are like those in other houses. Ideas we take into our heads differ hardly

1

more than foods we consume. Seldom is there reason to suppose more individuality in our thoughts than in our behavior and apparel. We happen to have access to our own physical and psychical quarters, and can shut the door on the rest of the world; but there is no mysterious cleavage between this subjectivity and what is objective or out in the open.

The sameness of human wishes in their most subjective state is made public on the screen of the movie, in the human-interest stories of the newspaper, in magazines and novels, in window displays and on billboards. Advertisers write the open text on æsthetics that all may read. They know that men and women are enough alike to want the same things, to admire the same beauty; and they are so sure of this that on it they stake their fortunes.

It would be idle to argue that each person has not a different idea of beauty, were not the illusion of uniqueness rather universal. People are richer or poorer in appreciation, but, as in their belongings, they are luxurious or lacking in similar things, so that their very differences are the same. Imaginations and predilections are as objective as hair and eyes, and equally dependent upon heredity and environment. Given a certain nature, education and experience, certain wishes will be inevitable which will necessarily be reflected in appropriate beauty. Precisely because variation is rare it is magnified. Each person cherishes what personality he has, and is glad that in being conditioned to seek his own he can reject what is foreign to him and call it ugly, though he is also happy to be like other people and to share their enthusiasms. There is less dispute about beauty than is often assumed, because most people accept the standards of their country and sex, class and set.

Æstheticians themselves are in surprising accord as to the nature of beauty and art. They usually agree that beauty is value and that art is the means of realizing value. They say that beauty lifts us out of our littleness to understanding of the meaning of existence. In beauty we see the finish and finality toward which our efforts tend, the poise to which our wobbly lives aspire. In beauty we behold our desire without ceasing to desire it, for the more satisfying beauty is, the more it arouses longing. The classic ideal of beauty is more calm, the romantic more vehement, while the modern tends to be wild and madcap; yet there is passion in the classic ideal, composure in the romantic, and some restraint in the modern, else none of them could be beautiful.

Because it is our nature to cling to the familiar and yearn for the strange, beauty must be woven of the known and the novel, the law and the prophets. There is nothing more beautiful than a sunset, and what is it but the colors of infinite long- ing suffused with peace? The effect of the stars is similar, their bright multiplicity evoking mani- fold aspirations, their shining unity assuring us of harmony. Akin to the beauty of sunset and stars is that of the sea, an illimitable expanse ever chang- ing, ever the same, in ceaselessly modified, inces- santly monotonous motion.

The beauty of nature is like that of art, inasmuch as all beauty is a human creation. Beauty is not an element to be found in the chemical formulas

4

of salt water and the atmosphere of evening, any more than it is discoverable in analysis of the pigments on a canvas. Beauty is value contemplated. It may be objected that the beauty of a work of art, in being determined for us by an artist, differs from the beauty of nature which is not fixed or even existent unless imagined by man. Those who believe that a work of art contains beauty within itself, however, will not put the question to a popular vote, but will appeal to the testimony of sensitive observers, the very persons who are most able "to find" beauty in nature. It is often held that because beauty in nature is analogous to that in art, nature must be the work of an artist; but then it must be admitted that man's works are also his work. Art and nature have the same beauty, whether we say that God makes both; that man makes both; that God makes man who makes both; or that man makes God who makes both.

It is impossible to establish a deep distinction between beauty and art, because whatever is characteristic of one is qualitative of the other. The only difference is that in beauty considered as art attention is called to the process of satisfying wishes by objectifying values; whereas in art regarded as beauty the important thing is the contemplation of values after they have been objectified. When we think of art, we are thinking of the skill by which beauty was produced; when we think of beauty, we are thinking more of the result than of the work by which it was achieved. But neither art nor beauty can appear without the other, because it is impossible to objectify value without contemplating the achievement of it, or to contemplate value without some thought of the effort by which it was realized. An artist cannot create a beauty that he does not appreciate as worthy of his work; and other people cannot appreciate the beauty of his achievement without admiring his art.

Every human being is an artist, because everything that he makes embodies wishes, and will be more or less beautiful according to our sympathy with his wishes and his power to objectify them. This view tends to make beauty ubiquitous, and there is a prejudice that beauty should be rare. But there is also a wide belief that beauty is everywhere for the eye that can see it. The universality of beauty, however, does not depend upon there being a theory to celebrate its epiphany wherever it appears. Any theory that does not clip the wings of beauty is unable to keep it from soaring and alighting where it will.

After realizing the potential ubiquity of beauty, it must be remembered that the probability of encountering it everywhere is slight, because beauty is not only that which is sought in the fulfillment of a wish—it is the value of that fulfillment as contemplated. This intellectual aspect of beauty keeps it from being too common. Everyone has wishes, but not everyone stops to consider and tenderly reconsider the values involved in their satisfaction. Life on the level of instinct or custom is not necessarily unæsthetic, but it is non-æsthetic. To create or behold beauty a person must be awake to values and not sleepily stumble over them.

Gulliver tells of seeing a machine for throwing letters of the alphabet into the air in the hope that they might chance to land so as to spell out an

7

epic like *The Iliad* or *The Odyssey*. But if men could produce books with such a machine, no more credit should go to them as artists than if their hands were guided through the motions of writing by Homer himself. It is impossible to carry through a serious work of art without intelligence, and without the persistence that comes only with organized habits. Lindbergh did not fly across the ocean by accident, and Byrd did not reach the polar regions by chance.

Neither can the beauty of such artistic feats be appreciated without intelligence. Appraisal of a beautiful thing is not possible on the part of one who does not take the trouble to know what it is or what it involves. Much that passes for æsthetic appreciation is spurious because often people merely happen to be "taken" with something that they call beautiful. If called upon to criticize it they would have to admit that they had simply taken a fancy to it. They would have no justification for their interest, no assurance that they truly liked the thing in question or that they would continue to value it.

When we are too easily pleased we are in danger of failing to appreciate beauty. That is why great art does not merely satisfy. It also arouses. To truly appreciate beauty the imagination must not out-reach reality, but reach out to ever-expanding ranges of it, and delve into ever deeper levels of what is near and familiar. A child is attracted first of all to what fills his immediate needs—his mother, his nurse, and his little belongings. Later he may be able to take similar interest in things adapted to the needs of others, through putting himself in their place. At last he may discover the highest beauty in dreams for the race, and find them embodied in his own children.

Chapter Two

ÆSTHETIC EXPERIENCE

THE æsthetic experience is not limited to appreciation of the fine arts, but includes the enjoyment of beauty everywhere. Anything that is regarded with deep satisfaction or longing, because it answers to desire, is beautiful. A doll, a dog, a hat, an automobile, may be valued enough to be contemplated as a thing of beauty. People are especially sensitive to values that appear in anticipation. The hopeful lover, the scientist on the track of a discovery, or the man eagerly awaiting his dinner, vividly looks forward to what is coming; and when it does come he is completely alive to its values. Even after he has been pleased, he may stay to think over the pleasure he has had, reluctant to leave his sweetheart, the laboratory, or the table.

An experience is æsthetic that is longed for, prolonged, and looked back upon for its intrinsic value. When something is regarded as beautiful, one can scarcely believe that it will come, cannot realize that it is there and cannot bear to think thát it has gone. When beauty is absent, it is present to the imagination; and when it is actually at hand it is delightfully unreal. The æsthetic experience occurs in every phase of living, whenever something desired enough to be a value is contemplated for its own sake. There is a tendency to think of the æsthetic moment as merely intermediary between desire and satiation—only a step toward a consummation that will enable humdrum activity to resume its mechanical march until a fresh need calls a halt before another desirable object. This is a militaristic nightmare of forced marching for the sake of more marching, stopping to plunder the values and ravish the beauties of every situation, only to plunge on afresh, drafting whatever will aid heartless advance, and trampling all else underfoot.

The lover of beauty is a conscientious objector

to this procedure, because to him value is to be contemplated for its own sake, not for that of ulterior activity. He may admit that wishes project values, and that contemplation of values leads to their attainment, but the lovely moment of contemplation, though it will not linger, is what he lives for. Æsthetic insight is for him the peak of experience.

Like a flower that is plucked, beauty seems to fade when it is attained, because then attention is drawn away to values unachieved. Other desires project images upon the screen of consciousness, causing the light of beauty to shift its focus and to follow the drifting wishes of the heart. But as often as the wishes revert, that transfiguring light will return to illumine a familiar place or face; for, like love, beauty has wings to fly away, and to fly back.

The seeker after beauty is not vainly on the go, trying to overtake a fleeting goal. Throughout his wanderings, like the pilgrim who rests in the Lord, he abides in beauty, because to seek beauty is to possess it. The æsthetic moment, arising in the midst of ordinary experience, may spread over the whole of it, enveloping it in beauty whenever we contemplate values. Even after the problem of achieving certain values has been solved, they may be contemplated as long as there is an echo of that problem; for the feeling of a need does not disappear as soon as relief comes, but lasts on, giving joy to success and triumph to victory.

When a ship reaches haven after struggling with a storm, the sensation of stress remains with the passengers long enough to increase the permanent value of *terra firma*. As long as one can recall an uncomfortable state, the value of release from it will continue to be enjoyed. A man who has come into good fortune will congratulate himself whenever he remembers his former adversity. A man does not tire of what he has, so long as he is aware of needing it. To remind himself of his discontent without it is enough to renew its charm. Things lose their appeal when they cease to fill a need, but a beauty that answers to a lasting desire is a joy forever.

Enduring needs insure the permanence of their

13

corresponding values. The daily recurring requirements of the body make food, clothing, and shelter eternal values. Man craves activity and rest for every capacity that he has, physical or mental. A gymnasium is valued as a place for exercise, but the beauty of a gymnasium is limited because it has facilities for only restricted kinds of exercise. Nature is more attractive than a gymnasium because in her fresh air man's legs and arms, mind and heart, function more freely; there is more to hear, to taste, smell, touch, and contemplate.

Art, like nature, is beautiful because of its opportunities for exercise and repose. Music is composed of expectation, disappointment, partial fulfillment, teasing delay, surprising gratification, distraction, titillation, blunt capitulation, , subtle repetition, elegant elaboration, unsuspected but inevitable termination. Architecture is constructed in the same way: weight pulling against weight, stress meeting strain, lines lifting lines that lower, bulk supporting bulk that sinks, one fall compensating another, so that gravity is conquered, here delicately, there boldly, now not at all, then but a little, and finally altogether. Similarly, painting is mixed of light and shade, surface and line, color and texture, depth and distance, all balancing, counterpointing, and harmonizing in a vibrant unity. Sculpture is molded of line, surface, and mass, till it rises like life from the earth and stands in a living equilibrium. Literature is all that these arts are, and more: it is their synthesis and apotheosis, for it vies with them in ministering to the body and surpasses them in serving the soul. Literature is the architecture and music of volition, the vivid painting of feeling, the quickened sculpture of thought.

In all art the principle is the same: the dexterous adaptation of means to ends for the enhancement of life. Wherever this adaptation is accomplished there is art. A distinction is often made between the "fine arts, which call for the exercise of taste and imagination, and the useful, industrial, or mechanic arts, or arts of utility, which require chiefly manual labor or skill,"[1] the former being designated the sphere of the artist, the latter that

[1] *Students' Standard Dictionary,* Funk & Wagnalls.

15

of the artisan. As Mr. Dewey says,[1] such a distinction is invidious, because it sets aside fine art as final and consummatory and reduces other art to the menial and initiatory, as if one dealt solely with ends, the other merely with means—something impossible, since art of any kind can arise only in so far as there is integration of means and ends. Indeed, this integration *is* art.

To limit art to the fine arts is arbitrary. Few people will deny that there are some artistic products outside the so-called fine arts, and few will agree as to which are the really artistic works within the circle of the fine. It is better to go to the other extreme and say that every work of man is a work of art; for art is the production of beauty; beauty is that which delights in itself; what is intrinsically delightful is value; and man makes nothing that does not represent value. This does not imply that every work of man is great art, but that it is impossible to draw a line between the works of man, defining some as art, some as not-art.

[1] *Experience and Nature*, ch. ix.

16

Art is not outside life, a rival to it. Thoughts, feelings, and deeds of man are the stuff of art; its purpose their enrichment. The apparently external structure of art is internal to human life. The achievements of art, its complications and *dénouements*, take·place within us. However objective and detached it may seem, it has no beauty apart from its effect on us. Art is simply the refinement and perfection of human experience. We admire art because all that it does is done to us by some of us for the benefit of all.

Since art is the integration and arrangement of life, a street car is not fundamentally different from a symphony in function or purpose. Both are conducted for the enhancement of life, though both go unappreciated unless acute need for them is felt. A street car is beautiful if it is successfully designed to serve the need of cheaply conveying the public about the city. In so far as its purpose is incidentally to please the eye, its color and outline become important considerations, as they are in automobiles and buildings. So-called demands of the eye are real enough to enable people to en-

17

joy objects which have no other use than to be looked at. Objects which people enjoy looking at are truly useful in stimulating and soothing the whole body and personality through the eye. But when a long-awaited street car appears around the corner, regardless of its looks, it is hailed as a thing of beauty, the chariot of fire that it really is.

The telephone is also a work of art, and a passage from Marcel Proust will show how it can delight an æsthete. "We are like the personage in the tale to whom a magician, in response to a wish, causes to appear in ˙upernatural clarity his grandmother or his *fiancée*, in the act of turning the pages of a book, of weeping, of picking flowers, close to the spectator and yet very distant, in the very place where she really is. For this miracle to be accomplished we have only to approach our lips to the magical little disk and call— sometimes too long, I admit—the Vigilant Virgins whose voices we hear each day without knowing their faces, who are our guardian angels in the vertiginous mysteries whose doors they jealously watch; the omnipotent ones through whom the absent surge at our side, without our being permitted to see them: the Danaïdes of the invisible who incessantly empty, fill, and transmit the urns of sound. . . . As soon as our call has resounded, in the night full of apparitions upon which our ears open alone, a slight noise—an abstract noise —that of the distance suppressed—and the voice of the dear one addresses us. It is she, it is her voice which speaks to us, which is there. But how far away it is!"[1]

This is the æsthetic experience, in which aspiration and consummation, the two poles of life, are fused. Every work which brings about this experience is a work of art, be it street car, telephone, painting, or poem. Anyone who appreciates art can see this, and the best of art is that it gives this insight to its lovers, showing them the unity of life, and the folly of trying to confine beauty in an ivory tower. An appreciative person can see the fineness of "utilitarian" art as well as the usefulness of

---

[1] Proust, *Le Côté de Guermantes*, vol. i, p. 119.

"fine" art. He knows that there must be a bit of charm even in a tin cup, and some earthly use in satisfying the most ethereal thirst; that there is something fair about the fit, and something fit about the fair.

Wherever there is intelligent and delicate adjustment there is art: in devising tools and machinery; in developing government and religion, business, science and philosophy; in planning intimate and domestic affairs; and in carrying on intercourse with friends, as well as in the "fine" arts.

There is no life where there is no art, where there is no integration of forward look and achievement, or no tension between effort and fulfillment; for there could be no appeasement without appetite or appetite without appeasement, because when one swallows up the other, the other swallows it. When a desire is completely satisfied it fades away, but so does its satisfaction. Life ceases to crackle between its poles when these are approached too closely, and art loses its charm when its arousing aspect is absorbed by its quieting quality, or when its soothing effect is drowned by its exciting element. Art must be a blend of stirring feeling and circumscribing form, a union of the vital and the shapely. Form without feeling will freeze, feeling without form will explode, as life without zest will atrophy, and life without rest will fail.

Art cannot be mere impulse without direction, or bare order and regularity without activity to be ordered and regulated. Art always derives vitality from a desire, and takes shape in working out a means of satisfaction. Ships have different shapes, owing to the different needs for which they are built, though there are variations of pattern adapted to the same general purpose. Steamships are less fair than sailing-vessels only when unfairly judged by the standards of the latter; and Conrad, who knew both, found equal romance in them. If modern steamers are more beautiful than early ones, it is because their design is better suited to the demands upon them.

Since some demands upon ships are sentimental, those fueled with oil must carry funnels like the old coal-burners. The requirements of sentiment are so important in many works of art that a failure to take account of them would be fatal. That is why the graceful structure of a skyscraper must be sepulchered in stone, steel furniture must seem to be of wood, and electric lights resemble candles. The shocks of progress must be cushioned and paved away, that the iron shod future may tread softly on the bare toes of the past.

But whoever has thrilled to watch steel girders, with men astride them, swing into place on a high building, or has trembled beside the rhythmic engines of an ocean liner, responsive to human fingers, will not regret the past or believe that in the days of the Pyramids or Cathedrals it was any truer than today that life is caught up and focused by art, enabling us to realize all at once man's yearning to satisfy inordinate ambitions, and the miracle of their satisfaction by art. Every work of art, knife or picture, vase or street car, cries a need and celebrates its relief. In all art the bitter neces-

sity and poverty of man are objectified and meta-
morphosed into adjustment and luxury by imagination and labor. In one suspended breath art mirrors
the full gamut of existence, the beginning, the end,
the acme.

Chapter Three

THE MYSTICAL QUALITY OF ART

ONE who approaches life as art may be called a mystic. To him life has infinite interest. Blots and blanks simply challenge his ingenuity for making everything fit. He is one who feels the ineffability of the ineffable. He is moved to wonder by the miracles all about him, the letters from God, as Walt Whitman said, signed by God's name, which he finds in the street, and does not pick up, because he knows that there will be more of them wherever he goes, forever. He sees directly in life the possibility of all that is mirrored in art, and tries to share his vision with others. He could not keep it to himself if he would. The thrill of it would show in his eyes, his voice, his walk, and would be the real burden of his conversation, no matter what he talked about.

There are men and women like that, the very thought of whom is refreshing, whose tones are music, whose words are poetry, who are always interesting because of their interest in everything. In their presence nothing is commonplace. A glance from them, a laugh, and we are dazzled by the splendor of existence. They speak our language, but with idioms and accents that make it strange. They see our world, but as if it were just discovered. They call us by our names, but evoke selves we had not known. To enter their kingdom we must be born again. They laugh at grown-up gravity as we smile at childish seriousness; but we envy their laughter and they pity our smiling. We are weighed down and fenced in, while they sparkle with fun that sets them free. They revel in the furniture of earth and the choir of heaven as a child delights in his toys. Like Shelley, they play with the stars and get between the feet of the horses of the sun.

They rarely get hurt, and when they do they are grateful, as if for a gift. Yet they are sympathetic with suffering, and excel in comforting the afflicted, because they are able to transmute the pain which paralyzes into the pain that stimulates. They believe that hidden within ugliness there is always beauty, for those who are patient and inventive enough. For mystics the very presence of a problem is earnest of a solution.

But the mystic is not radically different from other men. His are simply human traits which may be more pronounced in one man than in another without ceasing to be common. We all know that for every lock there must be a key, and are all subject to the temptation of the mystic to be content with knowing that there is a key instead of hunting for a lost key or making a new one. To know that a thing can be done is easier than knowing how to do it. Many men dreamed of flying before the Wright brothers invented the airplane. The talking-machine was a familiar idea before Edison made one. Countless people aspired to fill the need for poetry, music, and song before Caruso, Beethoven, and Shakespeare. Still we can imagine new triumphs. Like the mystic, we all have some notion of what is lacking, or we could not tell when the right thing is found. With him we may believe that nothing can be altogether absent, because the most remote thing is linked up with the present or it could not be imagined. We may also believe it impossible to corral at once all the implications of anything. When we make the attempt we are overcome as much as any mystic, if not as rapturously.

A person who thinks that he sees more deeply into the relatedness of life than other people must convince them that he is not deluded. The power of persuasion is the certificate of genius. No questions are asked of ordinary mortals, but he who has visions must show his passport from the abode where the eternal are. People are suspicious of mountebanks, but cannot help admiring men like Astor and Rockefeller who repeatedly solve real problems, proving that they see connections where others are blind. Such insight belongs to a Rachmaninoff or Manet; to a Houdini who can loose bonds that would hold anyone else; to a Burbank who can improve on nature. Because they actually free us from custom these men are not like those

27

who have only dark sayings to show for their vaunted clairvoyance.

Like children listening to a fairy tale, we marvel at artists who recreate the world for us. They need not be great and famous. As wonderful as any to admiring eyes are sailors shining brasses; washwomen hanging what were dirty clothes, sweet and clean in the sun; bootblacks putting polish where there was none before; all who purify and brighten —ash men and garbage men, street-cleaners, chimney-sweeps, and the inventor of the incinerator.

The mystical quality of art inheres in its power to erase labels and teach us to look for beauty wherever value can be contemplated. Appreciation of any art should lead to recognition of its attributes or their counterparts in any other art; and wherever such characteristics are confronted the presence of art should be confessed. It is taken for granted that a person familiar with one of the "fine" arts should be sympathetic toward the others. Usually it is admitted that literature, though not on the roster of the fine, may be as fine as painting, sculpture, music, or architecture, when prac-

28

ticed with as much skill and feeling as they. Fineness is often conceded to the dance and the theater, and sometimes to the movies. People with mystical sympathy see no reason for putting any use of knowledge and ability beyond the pale of art that may be fine. Where sensitive intelligence is at low ebb or absent, they supply it themselves. Tin cans on a dump-heap may reflect for them colors that painting has taught them to love.

> The angels keep their ancient places;—
> Turn but a stone, and start a wing!
> 'Tis ye, 'tis your estrangèd faces,
> That miss the many-splendoured thing.[1]

Appreciation, even of beauty produced by another, is not passive. To see beauty anywhere, regardless whether anyone has seen it there before, is to create it, whether the creation ever be copied on to canvas or into a book, though one can hardly help communicating a thrill. Every intuition of beauty is a work of art overcoming some judgment of ugliness. Beauty is elusive and escapes when we

[1] Thompson, Francis.

29

try clumsily to capture it, though it may smile again when we are deserving. Then we know that it must have hovered near, invisible because we lacked the wit to win it back.

There is none so dull that he does not discover beauty now and then, yet most of us are prey to ennui because we keep forgetting insight we have had. We come to take for granted our achievements so that we cannot contemplate their value. Street cars seem commonplace when we see them every day, though they will acquire charm for everyone when they are as remote as vehicles in Dickens. We often see life as art when it is far away or long ago, and when we stand back from it in imagination. But to feel life's beauty lapping against the feet of the present is a mystical experience to thank God for.

After artists of all kinds have shown that there is loveliness under the most unlikely guise, we must realize that no matter how much others may help us, we must make the effort to see beauty for ourselves. The most imposing effects of man or nature cannot save us from boredom without our coöperation. Even when we have made gains against the ugly, they must be renewed, lest they ooze away. We cannot bask forever in the glory that was Greece. To appreciate what that was we must reënact it, for the only way to be like the Greeks or any men who lived vividly, is to seek fresh triumphs of our own.

Every artist is discontented with former conquests, and all art is romantic in the sense of invading new realms. Beauty can camp in the same citadel for centuries only when defended by art vital enough to make constant sallies against encroaching ugliness—art that retains the romantic quality. Work that is romantic in a derogatory sense fails to discover values, and fans unfounded enthusiasm. From its feverishness we desire escape to something that does not pump up applause, because it derives genuine excitement from rendezvous with novelty.

Victor Hugo, instead of attempting to restore the old upholstery of fiction, went where none had ventured—to the red mouth of Fantine, Cosette with her broom, and Jean Valjean pursued through

31

the sewers of Paris. Rodin broke from the cult of antique sculpture to stretch marble with new life. Cézanne turned attention from the old story-interest in pictures to "abstract" form. Einstein and all the artists of science are discarding or revamping classic formulas to reveal strange universes. John Dewey is reconstructing philosophy, enabling us to throw off ancient ways of viewing existence that prevent appreciation of values in the present. Everyone who lives with an artist's vision sees the world as if on the first day.

An artist is aquiver with the adventure of living, even when he says that it is not worth while. The disenchantment of Anatole France and Santayana is belied by the whimsicality flickering about the edges of their most solemn pages. The fun that is in them bubbles up from a deep love of life. The pessimism of Thomas Hardy, unrelieved by humor, is apparently a different matter. But his bitter resentment against the lot of man could arise only from conviction that human existence might be better than it is, from a vision of values so conspicuous to him by their absence that he continually reflected them for contemplation, though reversed as in a mirror. He has already persuaded the world that Tess was a pure woman, helping to make it a better place for women like her. Through his art inspiration is drawn for efforts, increasingly successful, to save obscure people like Jude from tragedy. His desolating conception of fate, the response of a sensitive nature forced to give up the notion of Providence, steels the determination of equally tender but more enlightened spirits to make man the captain of his soul.

That man can be anything of the sort is ridiculed by literary folk who are still under the spell of outworn science. Their opinion would be negligible were they not able, through being articulate, to mislead many readers into thinking that the world is no more interesting than molecules in motion, though how it could be merely that is interesting enough. Theodore Dreiser confesses that to him it is all a welter, that he can make nothing of it. Men like Aldous Huxley and Ernest Hemingway are more or less in the same predicament. Unlike Thomas Hardy, they fail as artists in so far as they lack the mystical sense of beauty sleeping everywhere. They are baffled men who believe that values are illusions, and seek consolation in feeling that we all are helpless cogs in meaningless machinery.

But machinery is never meaningless, because it always has a purpose. Nowhere does a wheel turn against man's will. Machinery is simply the means whereby human purpose is carried out, as John Dewey would say, who is a harbor light for those tossing in futility: "All life operates through a mechanism, and the higher the form of life the more complex, sure, and flexible the mechanism. This fact alone should save us from opposing life and mechanism, thereby reducing the latter to un-intelligent automatism and the former to aimless splurge."[1] Where there is life there is value, the projection of hope; and all that is necessary to ful-fillment is the perfection of machinery, which is but another name for art. The artist does not despise means and then bemoan the loss of ends; or exalt means without consideration of ends. He

[1] Dewey, John, *Human Nature and Conduct*, p. 70.

34

solves problems by fitting together means *and* ends. As a good workman he feels that it is an art to make tools, he uses the best he can get, and knows that the most powerful instruments are new ideas. They are the chief means by which beauty can be extended and secured.

The artist is a mystic in believing that beauty can be found anywhere; and like the great mystics, who founded orders and built hospitals, he does not lazily wait for it to come down from heaven, but works and fights for it. When the ugly rides against him in the panoply of ignorance, marshaling an army of hard facts like the ten thousand iron chariots of Sisera, he does not flinch. He does not fool us with false safety in the face of danger; he does not pretend that without art life is always friendly and beautiful. But he is confident that with art man can remake a leaky, draughty existence: build dykes against floods, cut canals through continents, wipe out disease; and overcome ugliness in all its forms, discovering everywhere the stuff of dreams, the texture of the garment of God.

35

PART TWO
FINE ARTS

Chapter Four

THE MOVIES

ALL art sways between dream and reality, supported by both, like a suspension bridge over which life travels back and forth. Fine art may belong nearer one end (though that is neither for nor against it), but would fall away if separated from the other. Even our dreams are not wholly disconnected from our days, and art that we could not contemplate awake would not make us dream. Because movies project the real world, people like their make-believe. The movies are the most popular of the fine arts because they stay nearest reality. Movies that venture far from familiarity are as unpopular as abstract painting, music, or writing. Any degree of banality may be reached by any of the arts, but the movies hardly ever leave the street.

39

It may be unfair for those who need a more refined art to condemn the ordinary movie as coarse when it provides the glamour that most lives require. But people who dislike the movies fear that they are lowering the tone of modern life in general. They see the trail of the serpent in magazines and newspapers, all with the same pictures of what is called unusual, and an old story shouting from their headings. The radio is first cousin to the movie, because people cannot help associating moving pictures with what is heard from the loud speaker. Most music, whether on the radio or not, is dance music that one cannot listen to without seeing the movie world of smart people gliding through luxury.

The attributes of the average movie are expensiveness and sensuousness, low humor and sentimentality. It reduces the complexity of life to a few conventional feelings which are registered in set gestures. It shrinks human nature to stock characters in expected situations which are explained by rubber-stamp captions held on the screen long enough for a first-grader to spell them out aloud.

But child-like people must be instructed now, the same as ever, by pictures as long as they cannot read without the aid of pictorial illustration. They are given pictures by the mile by men who give the public what it wants, satisfying naïve wishes in a painless way. The movies have been supported largely by immigrants who have found in them an answer to their problems, what they sought in life and hoped to find in America. Hence the continued representation of Indians and the Wild West, the display of wealth and the happy endings. The movie in its pictures all but materializes the daydreams of the masses.

It calls to its aid and incorporates in itself other arts that by themselves might be baffling to the public. To people who lack the intelligence or training to delight in abstract forms, many of the patterns which music constructs are dim and shapeless. To persons incapable of enjoying the play of light and shade, the balance of masses and the poetry of lines, painting must seem trivial. To the unsophisticated (and most of us are that) a painting is what it represents. Since it can well represent only one moment, which seldom has any connection with the canvases hung near it, painting appears woefully restricted when compared with the moving pictures that unfold a complete story and illustrate it throughout.

Paintings of landscape and the nude are almost the only ones that most people will linger over without hurrying on to something else, because they offer refreshing glimpses of values always longed for and too often inaccessible to contemplation. Since popular interest in pictorial art is concentrated in two subjects, it is not strange that the contemporary trend in painting away from representation toward abstraction, even in these subjects, should be discouraging to most men. They have learned that even when a painter still tries to bring nature to town, his effort must seem feeble compared with the ease with which a movie camera can range from Greenland's icy mountains to India's coral strand; empowering anyone to see the breathing of a forest in the moonlight, the sparkle of sunshine on the water, the shades of evening, and the miracle of dawn.

In popular opinion sculpture as well as painting is outdone by the movie in the revelation of human forms in almost all their shining nakedness. Keyserling remarks that were we able to enjoy the sight of harmonious bodies all about us, like some African tribes that he visited, we should have no need of sculptors. The movie nearly puts us in that situation, and many people naturally would rather see dazzling nudity as if in the flesh than in stone or pigment.

Since the movie takes over the static arts of painting and sculpture, giving them its movement, it is not surprising that it should domesticate the temporal art of music. To the lover of music its charm is largely the intellectual one of following its formal structure, but most people know only its sensuous thrill and the imagery aroused by it. The opera supplies visual objects to take the place of the vague imagery which accompanies music in most minds. But the richest opera company does not tap the resources of the movie in providing visual phenomena, and the movie is making the auditory domain its own.

43

The originator of the "close-up" and the "fade-out," and producer of the first "talkie," Mr. D. W. Griffith, has said: "The synchronized talking picture combines all the rhythm, flow, and action of the silent movie with the talk of the stage, and has the added advantage of close-ups and perfectly attuned music. For that reason I am sure that the legitimate stage and the silent picture will be things of the past within five years."[1] But the assumption that a composite art will surely win out over a simpler form that it has taken into itself is unwarranted. The opera has not threatened to supplant the stage, and the synchronized talking picture at best would have the same relation to the stage as a super-opera. Contemplation of values in combination is not necessarily more satisfactory than appreciation of them separately. Adding to what is pleasing in itself may only mar it.

As the silent picture was being perfected the movies were thrown back into crudity by the coming of the talkie. The finish with which "The Last Laugh" (with Emil Jannings) was produced by

[1] The *Chicago Daily News*, February 21, 1929.

the Ufa Company seems impossible now. It achieved such eloquence by silent means that captions could be dispensed with; but the "all talking" has talk where even a caption would be superfluous. The fun of hearing pictures speak makes unimportant the appropriateness of what is said, as formerly the fascination of seeing pictures move made the significance of their movement irrelevant. When people become accustomed to sound from the screen they will demand that it have more point; and no one can doubt that difficulties in the art of reproducing sound will steadily be overcome.

Improvement of the movie may not be a boon, since perhaps it already is too successful in fulfilling wishes. When desires are satisfied lavishly, without effort, they may be in greater danger of being smothered than when they are suppressed. The movie not only fills in dreams vividly, but does people's dreaming for them. Because literature still requires the reader to interpret its pages, the story-teller's art is being usurped by the movie, which unfolds narration before the eyes, enabling anyone to see the action itself instead of symbols in a book; sparing even the trouble of turning pages, and leaving the public nothing to do but to sit still and take in. Sometimes literature seems like a crippled old beggar woman imploring people to feed her out of the charity of their imagination, compared with the fresh young muse of the movie who bountifully gives them all that they might have imagined and adds more. Many people who would never have read it were entranced by the movie version of *Dr. Jekyll and Mr. Hyde*; while those who had read it had not suspected the magnificent shivers it would send down their spines *to see* John Barrymore change from the handsome doctor into Mr. Hyde.

Ben Hur was better as a movie than as a book, even for imaginative readers; and *The Three Musketeers*, with Douglas Fairbanks as D'Artagnan, retained a trace of the original. Spectacular action is none the worse for being filmed, but great stories suffer when presented, as they usually are in the cinema, as nothing but violence and passion. People who appreciate good books as their authors wrote them will seldom find them improved in the movies, no matter how well satisfied other folk may be. An experience or two like seeing Tolstoy's *Anna Karenina* traduced as "Love" (with Greta Garbo) is enough to explain a book-lover's scorn for the silver screen.

It may be that after exhaustively going over the obvious features of life the movie will be forced, in search for novelty, to investigate something subtler. Movie patrons, like all people, want something more than they are used to, and in so far as movies represent that "more" they must stand for the ideal. Because a thriving art objectifies wishes, when movie-goers begin to desire what is not in the movies, it will shortly appear there. Movies to some extent arouse and lead the public, but art must not go too far ahead of its audience to be appreciated, or lag too far behind; because when it fails to fill a need, when it does not objectify values that people care to contemplate, it ceases to be art. In doing the same old things over and over, the movie often forfeits the interest of forward-looking people and in their eyes jeopardizes its title to art. Paradoxically, the movie at its worst may foster æsthetic experience in an artistic person by compelling him to substitute his own imagination where none is evident in the film; and the movie at its best may challenge a thoughtful man to heighten his perception beyond the plane reached on the screen.

Any movie abounds in things that fascinate a metaphysical mind. There seem to be solid objects projected where we think we know that there are none. Does the same illusion obtain all about us? for there is nothing in any actual experience to show whether we are in the presence of a persistent entity or not.[1] There is seeming motion in pictures that we believe to be only a series of static photographs, for the movie camera is as incapable as any other of catching movement in the act. Whatever it gets is stationary. The faster and more accurate any camera is, the more clearly immobile is the object that it pictures. A blur that looks like motion is only the confusion of two or more exposures of something motionless. When films are reeled

---

[1] Cf. Russell, Bertrand, *Philosophy*, p. 119.

off, the spectators unconsciously supply the transition from one picture to the next. Perhaps they do the same thing in "real life." All motion may be illusion, as Zeno proved it was. If the camera snaps a man with his foot raised in walking, the foot must be exactly where it is, and not elsewhere. If the next exposure shows the foot in a different position, again the foot cannot be where it is not. If it is at B, how could it have been at A? And how will it ever get to C? The camera does not tell. It always finds men as motionless as rocks. Yet they must step lively when the camera blinks, like children playing the game where they steal away from the goal-keeper while his eyes are shut and stand still when he opens them.

A philosopher in the twilight of the cinema cave will be thrilled with the possibilities of motion while apparently entertained by a race between an automobile and a train. Like Galileo in church, watching the swinging lamps and reflecting on the laws of falling bodies, he may speculate concerning the difference between fast and slow motion. Everyone senses the excitement in this question when the film is greatly retarded or accelerated. Then the movie becomes a popular demonstration of relativity. As more people operate their own movie cameras, philosophical amusement will become general. In showing family pictures in the home it easily happens that the reel gets into the projector the wrong way, so that the children on the screen seem to slide up the hill that they slid down, and snowballs fly back to the hands that threw them. This can hardly fail to provoke reflection on the reversibility of succession in space and its irreversibility in time, and the dependence of both time and space on motion.

There is small excuse for being bored with a movie, because one is either absorbed in its obvious features or is not. If not, one is free to explore its recondite aspects, which are unlimited. While his neighbor is occupied in reading a caption, a man who has read it in a flash has time to consider the composition of the last scene as if it were a painting; to think of Einstein or listen to the music; or think of the kind of music he would like to listen to; or reflect on the concentration of his neighbor.

A man who is not satisfied with the charms of an actress may consider her shape as an example of the "significant form" which some æstheticians write about, that is supposed to afford abstract geometrical interest, albeit embodied in the flesh of a movie actress. He may think of her as a statue or as a figure in a painting. He may appraise the way she is dressed, as he would if he saw her in a shop or in the street. There must be at least as much to watch in a movie as there is in the casual movement outside a hotel window, which is always interesting enough to keep loungers gazing out contentedly for hours.

But if art fills a need in life, a movie is not very artistic which offers only what anyone could perceive without it. In so far as we are forced to organize material for ourselves, and have to supply form and significance, we are not in the presence of art other than that of our own creation. A work of art may leave something to the imagination, and invite interpretation, but it brims over with meaning. A man of wit can amuse himself. He can compose a good sermon while hearing a poor one.

He can derive superior thoughts from a worthless book, or come away refreshed from a wretched movie. But art takes a man under its ægis and fills him with wonder. Instead of forcing him to amuse himself to keep from being bored, art enthralls him with beauty.

The ordinary movie, however, entrances countless people, and is for them a satisfactory art. It is popular for the same reason that it lacks favor among the sophisticated, namely, that its dreams are not far fetched from material reality; though the "little cinema" movement interests the most fastidious, showing that there is nothing intrinsically crass about the movies, that they can be refined when refinement is demanded of them. No art can do more than provide its patrons with values that they wish to contemplate. The way the population flocks to see almost any moving picture is proof that by popular vote the movie is queen of beauty.

Chapter Five

THE THEATER

THE theater, to regain its ancient place, must become democratic like the movie. There is no reason why it could not be popular in price and comfort without lowering its standard. The craving to see people "in person" would empty any movie audience into the theater, were it accessible, attractive, and eager to please. The theater must learn from the movie to become less snobbish in its very architecture. Mr. Moderwell says that the way in which most theaters are built "is both bad ethics and bad art. It prejudices the effect of the drama among the rank and file, whose approval the Greek tragedians held equal in value to that of the rich. To build theaters in which cheap seats are acoustically, optically, or hygienically bad is an insolence in a democratic age."[1]

[1] Moderwell, Hiram Kelly, *The Theatre Today*, p. 31.

The theater might be subsidized by a public, like the New Free Folk Stage of Germany. Low-priced tickets are feasible when the theater is assured of maintenance without having to gamble on the box office. Big theaters might follow the example of the little theaters in building up a regular audience of dependable taste. The theater then would be more in the position of the opera, in having a repertory of plays of established merit which could be repeatedly produced with increasing finish, that people might hear over and over, their enjoyment enhanced with each repetition. A new piece could be presented now and then with some notion beforehand of the attitude of the audience; and the public could come to it with confidence in its value, after long experience of satisfaction at the theater. The Théâtre Français and the Odéon in Paris are like that, and there might be such a theater in every city. It would be as reasonable to support the theater, in part at least, by taxation as to have publicly maintained schools, universities, and libraries.

The potentiality of the theater for the education

and refinement of the people is incalculable. The theater may be an engine of enlightenment as well as of entertainment. It can widen our sympathies, shedding a kindly light on characters who had been foreign to us, so that we may think of them as friends. Having seen "Porgy" or "Abraham's Bosom," we must have more compassion for the Negro. Having witnessed "The Weavers," we must be less complacent about economic inequality. On the stage even our enemies can be presented as human. Perhaps we had fought against them, only to discover later, in the theater, that they were just like us.

Playwrights have broken away from the dogma that only a few themes are dramatic. They are proving that almost any subject can be dramatized, and trivial clockwork plots are being discarded from the serious theater as well as from high-grade novels. People who enjoy novelists like Dostoyevsky and Proust could not care for a play with set situations, a handful of motives, and two kinds of love. But now the theater is making use of the

55

same variety and complexity of life as the highest literature.

The theater need not lag behind the movie in taking advantage of recent developments in painting, music, and dancing, in addition to inventions in lighting and stagecraft. The theater may become a synthesis of all the arts. As Mr. Moderwell says, the theater may take the place once held by the church as the one institution "universal enough to find a place for every contribution of value which men, small or great, can bring to it."[1] Should the theater succeed in representing all human interests, the church could not rival it, because then the two would be the same thing, as they were in the Middle Ages, when plays were given by the church as part of its drama of salvation. If the movie threatens the existence of the stage, it is only because the theater has been slow to recognize the power that it might have today. When the theater awakes, it is more likely that the movie will be made ancillary to the stage than that the stage will be supplanted or assimilated by the

[1] *Loc. cit.*

screen. The movie, even the talkie, is seriously handicapped by not presenting real people, alive and breathing right before our very eyes. The theater will be saved by the deep, abiding passion to watch and hear actual persons.

Nothing is more interesting than to watch other people. Only a few studious souls find anything like the same interest in books or pictures, and, unless they have become crabbed, they are relieved to look up and see human beings or listen to them speak. Because man is a gregarious animal, with a craving for companionship, especially when it does not involve him in complications, he always finds pleasure in contemplating his fellow-men. They are the part of the environment to which he must first of all be conditioned and adjusted. To get along in the world means chiefly to get along with other people. One must continually watch them to see what they are doing, and to anticipate what they will do next, for they are not stationary like trees and houses. The movements of men cannot be ignored like those of birds and clouds. Men are, of all objects, the most dangerous; and because we must be alert to notice signs of favor or displeasure in them, it is highly stimulating to be in the presence of other people. No contrast is greater than that between being alone and being with some one. To be alone is to be rid of reservation and caution; to be with some one is to be on guard. When two or more people come together, they become self-conscious and watchful; a tension is set up, and there is drama.

Drama is usually welcome unless one has had too much. Men, women, and children like to participate in it, or to be bystanders when it is going on. Often it is more fun to be a spectator than to be an actor, because the onlooker can enjoy the irresponsibility of solitude along with the excitement of sociability. This is the fun of the theater.

Drama off the stage is likely to be inferior, because trivial things are mixed up with important ones, and the acting is amateurish. People seldom are acute enough to say the right thing at the right time, or with proper intonation and gesture. They get too angry to think how an angry person should act, or they are too much in love to behave like lovers. They cannot stop when they come to the end of a scene, if neighbors or the police do not interrupt before they reach it.

On the stage everything can be planned to come off as it should. Spectators are thought of and provided with seats, which ought to be arranged so that they can see and hear better than they could in eavesdropping and peeking into other people's affairs. Scenery gives the mood of the action, while the lighting emphasizes what should be watched, and throws the rest into shadow. Costumes and make-up help the characters to look their parts and harmonize them with the setting.

If casual observation of ordinary folks is absorbing, money is well spent to see the most engaging persons that there are, who know how to talk and act when they are given something special to say and do. When we know that the actors are real people in the same room with us, actuality is introduced into make-believe. We feel genuine anxiety and eagerness about what they will do, forgetting in spite of ourselves that they will do nearly what they did last night and the night before. Pictures, even when they move and talk, can never be so exciting as living people who, after all, might do tonight what no one ever did before.

The theater is a difficult art because its material is human beings who cannot be handled with the mastery that is possible in working with a passive medium. An actor's emotions interfere with his intention, so that his facial expression, gestures, and elocution are never quite what they should be. Control of the face might be managed by use of the mask, as in antiquity, in the mystery plays of the Middle Ages, in the Japanese "No" dances, and in some modern experiments. The face, however, is such a small part of the problem that Gordon Craig has favored the substitution of super-marionettes for actors. Since their movements would be precisely as desired, they would lend themselves completely to any design.

Marionettes are an ancient theatrical form, and, though they have often sunk to Punch and Judy, modern marionette theaters like that in Zurich are giving new impetus to the theater. These wooden people, because they are not expected to be life-like, are surprisingly so, with an intensity surpassing mere realism; and are never distracted by applause or its absence. What super-marionettes would be cannot be surmised from puppets that are degraded to aping bad acting. But a thoughtful person who has watched Tony Sarg's marionettes must have been struck with their possibilities and have wished that they might be given better plays.

The rarity of good acting, however, is not sufficient reason for doing away with actors. Difficulty is the precondition of art. Without a problem, values cannot be appreciated, and the more problematic an undertaking is, the more beautiful its success will be in contemplation. Art is the overcoming of difficulty, and few realize how hard is the actor's art. E. H. Sothern has said that great acting is impossible when actors spend only a few weeks on one play before turning to another, and when they undertake "Hamlet" as blithely as musical comedy. To intone Shakespearean speeches requires as much training of the voice alone as to sing in opera. Nothing in the theater is more important than the voice, which should be educated to take into its tones the joy and sorrow that the race has known through the ages, in living, thinking, and longing. No effect is more poignant than that of a voice which can express what it is to live. We are fully aware of the meaning of life in speech tender with sympathy and understanding, like that of Alexander Moissi.

The Japanese might teach us to appreciate the seriousness of acting, since their actors belong to families of professional actors from generation to generation. Seami, a famous actor of the Japanese "No" plays, said that an actor must learn to imitate so well that he can become the thing imitated and not need to imitate it, because he *is* it. He said: "One must understand that in the gestures of the 'No' there is the essential and that which is derived therefrom. The essential is the flower, and that which is derived is the odor of that flower; like the moon and her shadow. If one firmly grasp the essential, one can obtain mechanically its derivatives. . . . Never imitate the derivatives, because it is not necessary; know that to imitate the essential is to imitate the derivatives."[1]

Marcel Proust's account of Sarah Bernhardt's supreme triumph in the "Phèdre" of Racine[2] shows that, whether or not she had heard of Seami, she practiced his theory. Proust failed at first to appreciate her talent, because he tried to abstract it from her rôle, which he had studied in advance, assuming that it would always be the same, no matter what actress took the part of Phèdre. "But that which I was trying to perceive outside the rôle was simply one with it." Sarah Bernhardt, whom he calls La Berma, was like a great musician "whose playing is become so transparent and filled with that which he interprets, that he himself is no longer seen and is no more than a window which opens to a masterpiece." Proust could distinguish the intentions of the other players, "surrounding their voices and actions like a majestic or delicate border," but La Berma had interiorized her efforts so that he could not "wrest from her

---

[1] Yamada, T., "L'Art du Drame Japonais 'No'," in the *Proceedings of the Sixth International Congress of Philosophy*, p. 442.
[2] *Le Côté de Guermantes*, i, pp. 43, 44.

diction and attitudes, or apprehend in the bare simplicity of their united surfaces, those effects which did not show at all, so profoundly were they resorbed therein. La Berma's voice, in which there did not remain the slightest loss in matter inert or refractory to the spirit, did not admit the discernment of that surplus of tears which one saw flowing over the marble voice of Aricie or Ismène (because they had not known how to imbibe it) but had been made delicately supple in its tiniest cells, like the instrument of a great violinist in whom one wishes, in saying that he has a beautiful tone, to praise, not something physical, but a superiority of soul." Her arms seemed to be raised by the verses themselves, with the same force by which they caused her voice to issue from her lips. Her bearing on the stage was based upon calculations that had lost their voluntary origin and had "melted in a sort of radiance in which they caused to palpitate about the personage of Phèdre elements rich and complex, but which the fascinated spectator took, not for a success of the artist, but for an endowment of life." Her very veils were

64

alive. "Voice, attitudes, gestures, and veils, were about that body of an idea which is a verse . . . only supplementary envelopes that, instead of hiding it, revealed more splendidly the soul which was assimilated and diffused in them."

Proust questioned whether La Berma's interpretation was merely a reflection of the genius of Racine. But in the modern play which followed "Phèdre" on the same program, a piece without any literary value, she was as sublime as in "Phèdre." Proust understood then that the work of the writer was for the tragic actress only a material, indifferent in itself, for the creation of her masterpiece. She was like a painter who might find the motif for two pictures of equal value in a schoolhouse without character and in a cathedral which is itself a masterpiece.

An actor can make everything significant, even inactivity. Seami says: "There is the pause during which one does nothing. This pause must be filled with intellect. Pause during the dancing, pause during the singing, pause during the speaking, pause during the imitation—it is necessary to be

65

very careful not to relax your intellect in any of these pauses. This continuity of intellect charms the spectator."[1] When not only the slightest words and movements are made expressive, but even the stillness in which they are set, like the night with its stars, we are made to realize the mystery of life, in which tiny things are edged by the infinite.

A great actor is not a poet's puppet. He makes "play-acting" so vital that drama is felt to be the essence of life. He shows that any part can be as dramatic as any other, proving the Stoic doctrine that it does not matter what our lot happens to be, if we determine to make the most of it. Then every man may be thought of as acting a part that he must interpret perfectly, since he is simply being himself. Everything is absorbing, seen as we see at the theater: it is unique, yet part of a whole; it is valued in itself and for its relations; it is reminiscent and portentous, freighted with the past and fraught with the future.

After we have learned that all the world's a stage and all the people players, it is our own fault

[1] *Loc. cit.*

if we are ever bored—a fault that can be overcome by going back to the theater for practice in taking the æsthetic attitude toward life. Even toward our own lives we can take the position of a spectator at a play when we need relief from the rôle of active participant. Subsequent activity derives advantage from an interval of detachment, but it is refreshing in itself to regard our own affairs as if they pertained to another. To the onlooker vicissitudes simply add interest. We must be careful, however, not to observe ourselves too coolly, since too much unconcern destroys the pleasure of life as surely as anxiety. The spectator must imaginatively participate in what he watches in order to appreciate it.

If the theater cannot enable us to take the æsthetic attitude toward the whole of life, at least it can help us to see appreciatively aspects of existence that otherwise we might never contemplate. Only in the æsthetic attitude, when we give attention to things just for themselves, are we truly aware of them. Most things, if they attract our notice at all, do so merely as clues to other things.

We glance at them as we do at traffic policemen, to see how they are pointing, and having got our direction we forget them. Ordinarily we look at things barely enough to read their indication. Because we must concentrate on their message for us, we have no time to take in more. We go through life like tourists watching our route numbers and looking for the big tree where we turn to the left, or the red barn where we turn to the right. We consider the sky for signs of rain, we heed the clock to see if we are late, we inspect the speedometer, the oil and gasoline gauges, and continually revert to the road ahead. If we stop to speak to people it is to inquire our way or to ask for the nearest filling station. Otherwise we should not get on. If we held up traffic to admire the policeman's uniform he would arrest us. If we got out to gaze at the tree or the barn or the sky, it would detain us. Nothing shall distract us from the road, and even the road we scan only as much as driving demands. But at the theater there is no route to devour attention.

At the theater for about three hours we are not

going anywhere. During all that time we have arrived. Ahead of us, receiving our full attention, are the things that usually we hurry by, placed so that we can admire them to our hearts' content. There we can realize how lovely a tree is. Though the tree on the stage is not real, it is more of a tree to us than the one outdoors that is only a sign to turn to the left, because in the theater we can reflect upon its treeness at leisure. The policeman on the street is a real one at the cost of hardly being a man, but the one on the stage is seen as a real person who happens to be a policeman. Outside the theater we seldom have time or opportunity to satisfy our desire to observe things and people. The difficulty of finding out as much about them as we should like makes an absorbing problem that accounts for the beauty of the theater where all the objects before us can be contemplated as values, not abstractly, but concretely and in person.

Having seen on the stage how interesting everything can be, we must retain away from the theater a sense that all existence is dramatic. With quickened sympathy we shall smile at the policeman who helps us on our way, and realize that there is more than surface significance in signposts, that each of them is symbolic of a universe amenable to human purpose. As we drive along we shall more often remember that wherever we might stop to contemplate what is at hand, we should have arrived at a place where there would be enough to entertain us for at least three hours.

Chapter Six

PAINTING AND SCULPTURE

APPRECIATION of painting and sculpture requires more sophistication than enjoyment of movies and the stage, because a lifeless, two-dimensional or colorless representation of values does not strike home as readily as embodiment of them in human form. The difficulty of controlling actual people masterfully, in so far as it cannot be overcome, is overlooked on account of the intrinsic interest in people as such; and it is always wonderful that they should be made to fit into a design. There are so few things that most of us can say or do just as they should be said or done, especially in relation to several other persons, that any patterning and stylizing of human behavior is delightful, be it no more complicated than military drill or correct deportment in the drawing-room. The curious

71

fact about paint and stone, however, is not that they should take definite shapes and keep them, but that they should ever simulate the plasticity of life.

Any approach to humanity in the outline of cloud or rock is as remarkable as for anything human to approximate the regular designs with which nature is rife. The convolution of a shell, the parallel ridging in the sand of a lake, the symmetry of a bird nest, the geometrical character of a crystal, a snowflake, a leaf, or a spider web, all arouse the wonder of man by their regularity and by incalculable deviation from their main rhythm. But man is a child of nature: his life solidifies in habit and custom, yet remains fluid enough to continue flowing and changing its channel. He notes the repetitions and variations in nature because both are so fundamental in his own make-up that he cannot think except in terms of sameness and difference, or ever think of one apart from the other, though he cannot even be sure which is which. Man likes movies and the theater because there he can contemplate his fellows; there he is held by the same interest that makes life interesting, while he cares less for painting and sculpture because they have less human interest; they have a different appeal that is more difficult to appreciate. It is surprising to find that, after all, painting and sculpture may be more like what he really likes than many a movie and play.

He gets excited about colored canvas and cloven stone when he discovers how human they can be, or more than human. Hues of flesh and contours of the body can be caught and kept as if alive. Movement and speech must be omitted, yet in one silent moment, prolonged perhaps forever, a painter or sculptor can pack as much activity and utterance as there might be in a cinema or a drama. To perceive the significance concentrated in painting or statuary takes keener faculties and more training than to understand what is drawn out on stage or screen; and those who have education and intelligence like to use them. Values are engendered and enhanced by difficulty; and while it were unwary to assume that a more difficult art is always superior, it is safe to say that usually it is less popular than an art easier to appreciate.

The relative unpopularity of painting and sculpture, as well as their charm for their devotees, is increased by their present tendency away from representation of human beings as such, or of the ordinary objects of human interest. For those who see the point, man's solidarity with the rest of the world is emphasized rather than denied by the ability to represent people and their affairs from a point of view not excessively anthropomorphic. When the power to make marble and pigment look like people is attained and taken for granted, it becomes fascinating to express human values in non-human guise, and to discover human interest in what is not obviously human. To hint at the shape of man through that of cubes, or to find in abstract forms a rhythm familiar to man, which only man could feel, may be more fun to the initiated than mystery plays and dramas of love.

To seize upon the significance of life seems more important than a vain attempt merely to reproduce exactly and completely what is already formed in nature. To communicate what is particularly interesting the plastic artist has always intentionally as well as unavoidably modified his model. This is as true of Phidias and Giotto as of Renoir and Rodin. The artist also has always used aspects of actual things in making conventional patterns, and even in "pure" decoration has never entirely lost sight of natural objects. While some modern artists are engrossed with *abstract* form, they must retain a semblance of real things or lose the abstract *form* that they are after;[1] because it is impossible to invent shapes absolutely new.

If it is sophisticated to appreciate abstract forms, it is naïve to deprecate the familiar aspect of life from which they are abstracted. Since art represents values, it must, in addition to rearranging and editing experience, try to preserve the original when it is cherished. Art is expected to reflect things that are already beautiful, to record moments perfect in themselves. In the neighborhood of our homes there are views that could not be surpassed; there are people of our acquaintance as

[1] Cf. Cheney, Sheldon, *A Primer of Modern Art.*

charming as any who could be imagined; there are events in our lives as tender and dramatic as could be fancied. We do not ask art to improve on these things, but to salvage them from oblivion, that we may keep them to muse upon, for they are bits of joy with which to build our happiness.

Beauty is the selection from life and the record of that which we love. Portraits of dear ones are beautiful when we are separated from them, or are likely to be. We want near us tokens of precious things we cannot have close by. Where man's treasure is, or has been, there his heart is, and his art also. In so far as we can sympathize with another's love, art expressing his feeling will express our own. Art is as universal as human nature; and because men have fundamentally the same needs and emotions, art which truly represents another's yearning will find response in all.

Painting and sculpture must not become too abstruse and enigmatic, because they are art, and art is not a private affair, but a language, a mode of expression whose symbols must be intelligible. Since signs get their meaning from social usage, a man cannot talk even to himself except in terms of converse with others. Phases of consciousness that he cannot convert into the coinage of a common terminology he can no more indicate to himself than he can communicate to others. An artist who apparently cares little for an audience is compelled to work as if for others in order to express anything to himself.

Choice of symbols and systems of symbols is necessarily guided by consideration of ease and sureness in communication. It is a matter of social convenience. To ask what style of painting or sculpture is truest is as meaningless as to ask which geometry is the only one. Geometrical problems might all be dealt with on the basis of Euclid's axioms, all painting might be done in the Dutch manner, and all sculpture in the Egyptian mode. But some problems can be handled more simply with Riemann's geometry or Lobachevsky's than with Euclid's; some subjects can be painted more conveniently in the Venetian way than in the Dutch; and some ideas can be expressed more suitably in Greek than in Egyptian sculpture. Any set of signs may be chosen as vehicle for any meaning, but those signs are best that most clearly convey a meaning to other people. What cannot be conveyed must remain subjective.

The significance of a picture or statue continues to be subjective, though it hover near many minds, so long as none of them gives it expression. When some one fixes it in color or stone a meaning becomes objective inasmuch as it could be exhibited to others, though it will still be as subjective as if it had never been objectified, to all those who have not seen it. Even to its creator a work is infected with subjectivity until some one else sees it as he does. An idea represented in a style that only half a dozen persons can appreciate might as well not have been depicted as far as others are concerned. Objectivity increases with the circle of people who respond, and the elusive quality that Cézanne strove to capture is now known to a large public.

Many people want beauty thoroughly prepared for them by the artist, and are content with the smooth marbles of Canova or the obvious canvases of Cabanel. Those with a taste more robust, while they may derive some enjoyment from the sweetness of Greuze, find more satisfaction in coarser stuff, including the roughage of Epstein. In the modern world we tend to reject softer forms, but, as people have always done, we like what we lack and value what we need.

We still like painting to transport us to nature unaffected by man and his works; or to exotic cities, amid scenes and costumes different from our own, where nothing is commonplace or colorless, where everything is a delight to the eyes, and through the eyes an excitement to the other senses; where poverty is picturesque, dirt and rascality are romantic, and luxury is glamorous. The tissue of our dreams, too illusory to linger over as we would, is caught up by the painter and woven into a magic web, filmy and fanciful as ever, but more real and permanent than the unlovely things we would forget.

When we are distressed by unhealthy living and disease, it is refreshing to see unblemished landscapes and nudes; but it is also encouraging to be shown unsuspected values in actual scenes and peo-

79

ple that had seemed far from ideal. For the revelation of charm in the dumps of a city, for the discovery of poetry in the roofs and romance in the alleys of dingy quarters, we must be thankful; and for the unveiling of loveliness in wretches whom beauty had all but abandoned.

To realize this we have only to remember Millet's "Man with the Hoe" and Rodin's "Old Courtesan." "The Smoker," by Van Gogh, also makes us stop and consider a person whom we might have passed by, for he is rudely dressed and probably untutored. When we see him through the eyes of the artist we recognize a fellow-being, as content with his pipe as we with our philosophy, and as wistful. He is as much himself as we are. His old hat and coat belong to him as ours do to us. He could not properly wear any others. Whenever we see such a man again we shall more likely think of him sympathetically, for a portrait like that establishes the dignity of common humanity as truly as any declaration of the rights of man. Sculpture like Rodin's "Citizens of Calais" or Saint-Gaudens' relief in memorial of Robert

Gould Shaw, has the same effect. We cannot look at the figures in these groups without being proud of the species.

It may be illusion in the beginning that makes a painter or sculptor see beauty where he does, but that does not matter if he have the power to persuade us that he is right. Since art is persuasion, in the end the vision of the artist cannot be illusion, because he makes his insight real and adds it to reality. But whenever an artist lacks faith in a meaning that transcends casual appearance, when he not only fails to convince us that he sees a glory in it all, but boasts of his failure and concerns himself solely with technique, he ceases to be an artist.

Excellence of technique and originality of vision are not necessarily incompatible, but often they seem to be. People who know little to say, but know a lot about how to say it, are likely to seek perfection in every detail, like Messonier in his battle scenes; while those who overflow with things to express are frequently incapable or impatient of nice execution, like children whose

81

drawings are more often fresh than accurate. Some vagueness, by way of actual or apparent incompleteness in a work, may contribute to expressiveness by imparting what further finish might obliterate—the strange agitation, the indicible excitement of inspiration as it came to the artist. For this reason the effort of an amateur may have more fire than the craft of an experienced artist who can carry out his intention to the last notch. It would be mistaken, however, to ascribe all haziness to lack of skill, since the impressionist painters have made indefiniteness a definite part of their technique, and since Michelangelo, who could chisel a statue right out of the rock without pottering with a preliminary model, achieved some of his most tremendous effects by leaving a face blurred in the stone.

This does not permit the pseudo-artist to pretend that he has a message when he is merely blundering. In the end intelligence is not deceived and will be content only with intelligent work. What delights the mind is more than the result of accident. Rodin says: "In truth, if the skeptics . . . knew what energy it sometimes costs an artist to very feebly translate that which he thinks and feels with the greatest force, they certainly would not doubt that what appears luminously in a painting or in a piece of sculpture had been willed."[1] Critics who occupy themselves solely with the technical aspects of a work of art, trying to exclude consideration of what the artist willed to express, pour the baby out with the bath. They try in all seriousness to talk about a "Madonna" of Raphael as if she were naught but color, light, line, and shade. They say that through the analysis and synthesis of these elements they appreciate a painting. If Raphael intended anything more it is wasted on them. Such critics might answer, as Croce suggests, by saying that anyone might have imagined a "Madonna" like that of Raphael, but that Raphael was Raphael through the mechanical ability to fix it on canvas, and that consequently it is technique alone that should concern the critic.[2] What a paint-

[1] *L'Art*, ch. viii.　　[2] Croce, Benedetto, *Estetica*, p. 12.

83

ing expresses, or whether it expresses anything, would be of no importance then, if it were well expressed! As Croce says, nothing could be more false. How can we judge the expressiveness of what is not thought of as expressing anything?

An ink blot allows as much exercise of analysis and synthesis as any painting, because it has as much abstract unity and variety, but we should not call it a work of art. It is not abstract geometric regularity by itself that makes representation of the human form or features pleasing.[1] If so, there would be no more pleasure in the sight of them than in the symmetry that might be found in a blot. Lipps concludes that man's body is not beautiful on account of its proportions, but that its proportions are beautiful because they are those of man, and are the vessel of human life.[2]

Nature is beautiful as the setting for man's activity, but the artist discovers interest in aspects of the environment beyond or beneath ordinary notice. As we follow him we feel that he is pro-

[1] Lipps, Theodor, *Ästhetik*, i, p. 103.   [2] *Ibid.*, p. 105.

jecting our life into ultra-human and infra-human realms, expanding our experience through sympathetic contemplation of new values that eventually become as human as any. Appreciation of scenery has been increased by painting from almost zero to the point where landscape is full of human interest. The artist expresses himself in everything he does, and because his personality can be equally appealing in all his work, he can make us feel at home anywhere.

Leonardo, who led the way to a higher valuation of scenery, finds the same response in nature that his charm elicits from men and women. The secret of Mona Lisa's smile is that it reflects the presence of Leonardo. Sitting before the most seductive personality of the Renaissance, she makes us feel toward her as he made her feel toward him, and his smile hovers on our lips. The spell of the landscape background is the same as that of Mona Lisa's face. No one ever smiled like that, except to him; and nature never presented that visage to any other. By seeing in nature the effect that he desired, and being able to paint it, he breathed his own

85

life into the setting as well as into the sitter. He communed with the world of rocks and trees as he talked with Mona Lisa, until, illumined with the smile he sought, there was the same light on the land as on her lips.

Chapter Seven

MUSIC

MUSIC can be as catchy as the movies, or further from popular representation of reality than abstract painting and sculpture, though when most remote it is still related to life. Schopenhauer said that music, instead of reflecting the surface of life, goes down to the elemental will to live. In abstracting from particular aspects of existence, music concentrates the nature of experience and offers for contemplation the essence of all values. All that man can feel or think in all manner of situations is manifested in music. What he has known is recalled to him, what he has not yet known, and what otherwise he might never know.

"An art that came out of the Old World two centuries ago, with a few chants, love-songs, and dances; that a century ago was still tied to the words of a mass or an opera; or threading little dance-movements together in a 'suite,' became in the last century this extraordinary debauch, in which the man who has never seen a battle, loved a woman, or worshiped a god, may not only ideally, but through the response of his nerves and pulses to immediate rhythmical attack, enjoy the ghosts of struggle, rapture, and exaltation with a volume and intricacy, an anguish, a triumph, an irresponsibility, unheard of. An amplified pattern of action and emotion is given; each man may fit to it what images he will."[1]

It is little short of magical that such an effect can be achieved with sounds that by themselves have no meaning, and that in combination might be expected to afford only sensuous gratification. Tones which are musical are so rare in nature that Gurney calls them exceptions to exceptions, and remarks on the wonder of the ear's capacity for the refined enjoyment of sounds that in the whole history of the race almost never have been heard. He says:

[1] Quoted from *Nineteenth Century Art*, by D. S. MacColl, p. 21, in *Ancient Art and Ritual*, by Jane Harrison, p. 234.

"We may even go further, and assert that the ear will not stand definite sound colour as part of its ordinary environment. The most musical note, if prolonged continuously, would weary us in less than a minute; and formless successions of such notes would be more irritating still. Compare looking at a sunlit marble wall for half an hour, and listening to a tone or a few changing tones without form."[1]

Since the sixteenth century great enrichment of musical forms has been made possible by the development of instruments, and has been demanded by the increasing complexity of society and personality which can be expressed better in instrumental harmony than in vocal melody. Melody and song are still listened to with pleasure, but, for the most part, modern values are rendered more satisfactorily when melody is taken up into harmony and the human voice is used as if it were an instrument.

In these days we usually think of music as produced by an orchestra. A few instruments playing

---

[1] Gurney, Edmund, *The Power of Sound*, p. 35.

without the rest are a small orchestra. Even a single instrument, if a sort giving the pleasure we usually ask of music, will be heard as a tiny orchestra producing harmony rather than melody. The instrument probably most enjoyed by itself is the pianoforte, because it combines in itself the possibilities of most other instruments—melody, harmony, gradations of loud and soft, and even color or the tone quality of different instruments playing together.[1] It may be that melodies played on the piano suggest orchestral instruments because certain types of melody are characteristic of certain instruments. A progression will suggest horns to almost anyone, whether played in that register of the piano most like horns in quality or not, merely because such a progression is (or was, before the development of valve instruments) characteristic of horns.

The performance of a great pianist or violinist may give even more pleasure than that of an orchestra, largely on account of the interest in seeing one man take the place of many, and because his

[1] Cf. Bekker, Paul, *Musikgeschichte*, p. 122.

music is felt to be more personal than that of an orchestra. Intimacy accounts also for much of the charm of chamber music. When a soloist plays with an orchestra, leading it and supported by it, he seems to be playing twice a hundred instruments, those banked around him as well as those packed in the box beneath his fingers. The ensemble becomes a medium for expressing his personality, and even the audience which he plays upon becomes part of the orchestra that is part of his instrument.

An audience is not content to hear a musical performer without seeing him. People like to close their eyes during a program, but they wish to watch as well as listen to the personality that attracts them. When drawn to a musician they want to know him better, and hope to see in him what they hear in his music. As he walks out on the platform they wonder whether he will work a miracle on this particular night, and search him for a sign with more than a thousand eyes. But there is no sign by which they may know what is to be vouchsafed. There may be nothing unusual when he begins to play. The whole evening there may occur nothing of the order expected, though it may flash out when they have ceased waiting for it. Slowly it may steal over them, in a way that could not have been foreseen.

A performer with insight into the living spirit of a composition cannot be sure that he will be able to feel it sufficiently any evening to transmit the full sense of it to an audience. He cannot rely entirely on technique. He must lay it aside to some extent, as in refraining from playing over delicate passages in order that he may play them freshly in public. He prays for an inspiration that will enable him to play better than he knows, but its coming is always unexpected, and when it is gone he cannot feel sure that it will return. He cannot depend on it, and without it the audience cannot depend on him. Hence the intensity of the moment when he appears, and the greater his reputation the more breathless the expectancy. He must be calm or be lost, but he cannot be too calm or he will be equally lost. He cannot be uneasy and he dare not be confident.

Unless the composer and the performer are the same person, it is only through the interpreting artist that the "creative" artist can consummate his work. The soloist takes up into himself the composer as well as the orchestra and audience, and the conductor also becomes part of him. If the performer merely followed the score he would be only the composer's instrument. But a score can never be merely carried out, because everyone who reads it must interpret it for himself, as in reading words or in responding to any signs. It is impossible to put everything into symbols, or they would not be symbols. Relativity of time intervals can be indicated: if one note is assumed to last a whole beat, another will be held half as long, another a quarter; but how long a whole beat should be can hardly be designated, even with metronome marks. The same is true concerning gradations of loud and soft. They can be marked on the score relatively but not absolutely. *This* must be louder than *that*, and softer than something else, but how loud or how soft cannot be told. The performer must decide for himself in this and more important things, so that a composition rendered by him will become his own, for better or for worse. The composer may be only a fair performer, but even if a great one there may come along a greater who will so play his piece that the graceful thing for the composer to do is to present it to him. People who thought that Tschaikowsky's "Concerto" was nothing wonderful were amazed when Horowitz played it. Rachmaninoff, after hearing Horowitz play his famous "Third Concerto," said that he would never play it again.

The musician presents values for contemplation by pleasing the ear, the organism as stimulated through the ear, and the whole personality as influenced through the organism. People would not like music if it did not give them something that they crave, and in so far as they have different needs they make different demands upon it. Persons with logical or mathematical minds in want of exercise, value the abstract structure of music and are likely to disdain others whose musical interest is not focused in the definite, structural part but rather in what is indefinite about it and subjective. Speaking for analytical folk like himself, Gurney says that the better one knows music the more one enjoys what is definite about it, and the more one is pained by failure to seize upon that. This is why a novice may like what baffles a trained ear, though he would not recognize what he likes if he heard it again, or notice the difference if, during a repetition of what he had liked, something else were substituted.[1]

Mr. William Pole points out, however, that musical structure is not altogether definite even for the composer, since he knows that combinations of notes that would be regarded as unpleasant on paper "will be tolerated by the ear, and will pass almost unnoticed, if at the time they occur some other element of musical interest is offered prominently to the mind. . . . In regard to harmonic progressions, we find that there is no physical reason why any one combination of notes should be preceded or followed by any other combination; but that an æsthetic feeling exists requiring the progressions to be united by some

[1] Cf. Gurney, Edmund, *The Power of Sound*, ch. xiii.

95

kind of relation which the mind can appreciate."[1]
If composition itself is guided by consideration of
what is not definite, "æsthetic feeling" which over-
rides rules, it is plausible that the enjoyment of
music would be influenced by indefinite feeling.
Mr. Pole does not say that tradition and conven-
tion in music should be disregarded, and he believes that there are some physical laws that always
must be obeyed; but he holds that for the most
part "the musical forms are really the outcome of
the composer's own art—the offspring of his instinctive perception of what is pleasing."[2] He asserts further that what the composer is really trying
to do is to touch the heart, to stir the emotions, to
"breathe into his music the breath of life and give
it a living soul." This is saying that the composer
himself is interested in what is definite or structural in music only as a means to arousing that indefinite, ineffable pleasure that Gurney scorns. Yet
in Gurney's own work there is this passage: "Any
individual, whatever his taste, who among the

[1] Pole, William, *The Philosophy of Music*, p. 296.
[2] *Ibid.*, p. 298.

tunes he knows discriminates those which give him pleasure from those which do not, will find it entirely hopeless to form any generalization of structural features which are present in the former and absent in the latter."[1]

To insist upon limiting musical enjoyment to what is definite in the structure of music is like narrowing the appreciation of literature to technical interest in literary form, as if *there* alone could be found the difference between good and bad art. Musical form is used by the artist as a means to an end, but in itself should never become the end. When it is suspected that the artist's purpose is to exhibit mastery of technique, credit is given him for virtuosity, but one feels that this in itself is a barren thing. We say that it is cold and soulless. What we miss is something indefinite, especially when the artist is perfect in what is definite.

If the more we know about what is definite in music the less we care for what is indefinite, then for most people ignorance is bliss, including the sophisticated critic who coolly misses the very ex-

[1] Gurney, Edmund, *The Power of Sound*, p. 164.

citement which the composer tried to communicate through his technique. All that any art can do for us is to facilitate contemplation of values that we crave. To give up what is good for us because it is not good enough for some one else is a foolish sacrifice, since nothing can be better for us or more beautiful than what we love. No one can know more about what music means to us than we do, no matter what our limitation. Sincere love of what suits us is the best preparation for appreciation of unknown loveliness, and the only protection against self-deception. Let us have any knowledge that will enhance our enjoyment of beauty, but in so far as we do enjoy it, let us know that whatever knowledge we lack is not indispensable.

It is enough to know that music gives a sense of security through its recurrent structure and provides excitement through its indeterminate features, thereby satisfying the two basic human wishes. The structure is the skeleton of music, holding together the rest of it which consists in the experience of auditory effort, met more or less remotely by the feeling of achievement and relief.

According to one's nature and education a particular composition may be too simple to arouse pleasant effort or too complicated to allow repose.

What we merely hear is the body of music. It has also a soul. To the physical audition of music must be added what Lipps calls its psychic resonance, its reverberation of the moods of life. He says: "We may know the overcoming of dissonance in many different forms. We experience the same thing when the sun breaks through the clouds, when a quarrel is smoothed over, when we are freed from material distress, when doubt is ended, when any inner conflict is settled. All phases of inner experience which may lie within the tone-stimulus are recognized in all spheres of our life."[1] In short, we find in music all our passion and peace.

People who realize this, but think they are unmusical because they cannot play an instrument, are more musical than those who can play but do not feel in music the significance of life. Music, though composed of sounds, is made of moods and

[1] Lipps, Theodor, *Ästhetik*, i, p. 480.

99

played on the heart. That is why Beethoven's deepest creation might take place when he was deaf. No doubt he heard sonorous qualities in his imagination, but æsthetic audition is not the same as ordinary hearing, though perhaps there is no more difference between the two than between the psychical and the physical aspects of any experience in which they can be distinguished. The roar of the city disturbs the inner peace, and music, in soothing the ear, lulls the mind as well. Music takes vibrations, the elements of noise, and makes them over, as art ever draws upon life for its effects. Even actual noises may be domesticated by music. There are sounds of trains and traffic in Honneger's symphonic poem of the locomotive, "Pacific 231," in John Alden Carpenter's "Skyscrapers," and in Gershwin's "American in Paris."

Whether it represents actual things or not, music objectifies all life, for life is consonance and dissonance—it is music. The music-lover feels that instead of reflecting the surface of existence, music gives an intensified experience of living by distilling the values of aspiration and consummation, which are the essence of happiness. Music offers in concentrated form the best that life affords— the opportunity to strive, to achieve, and to remember. Like life, music "is always nine-tenths memory or premonition, since what is given at any instant is only one tone or harmonious complication of tones."[1] It is in listening to music that we understand how every act and thought is reminiscent and prophetic.

The common notion is, however, that music cannot speak for itself. Popular music is always accompanied by words which supposedly express what is really meant. Also in hymn and oratorio words and music, voices and instruments, blend together and assist each other. In opera there are acting, dancing, and stage-setting, as well as song, along with the music of the orchestra. Hence the opera is often disesteemed by those who appreciate "pure" music. But a soprano's stunts are admirable, at least as acrobatics, and need not distract one altogether from the music. Even a buffo's antics may be enjoyed by people who can also follow the

[1] Edman, Irwin, *The World, the Arts and the Artist*, p. 82.

subtleties of a composer. It is an excuse for the grosser aspects of opera if they are all that some people like about it. If there is something associated with music that attracts persons who otherwise might not listen to it, that may be a step in their musical education, though only the first step. Many devotees of the symphony were once operagoers, and a large number of people enjoy the symphony, the opera, and popular music too.

Music which follows a series of theatrical scenes must usually forego the close unity of the symphony, but in its parts it may be as beautiful as any music, and occasionally it may have the large unity that Wagner sought. Opera music need not imitate closely what is happening on the stage, since through emotive association it can fit in with the drama and heighten the mood of a scene, as it can deepen the significance of a dramatic event in life, like a wedding or a funeral. The scene in turn helps to control the indefinite imagery aroused by the music, though that is just what some people resent.

Whatever the music we prefer, we miss its chief

value if we are content to be physically stroked and mentally caressed by it. Gurney scorns delight in trills and cadenzas, but that is innocent compared with receiving nothing but sensuous stimuli from music as a total situation. We should feel in music an expansion of personality, a regeneration of sympathy; but if we refuse to take this seriously our musical experience becomes sentimental and sensual. That is why William James said that after hearing a concert a man should give some expression to the kindliness kindled in him, lest it die, leaving him deaf to the music of music. He should obey the muse-inspired impulse and do a kind act, if only to give his seat to an old lady in the street car. Thus, in addition to psychic resonance, which is above the physical effect of music, there is a social resonance.

Music, as medium of feeling, is deeper than words, the language of reason (though words may be unreasonably emotional). Music plays more directly upon the emotions than literature which addresses itself chiefly to the intellect (though nothing could be more intellectual than the ab-

103

stract structure of music). Welling up from the bottom of our being, music expresses what could not be put into words—our deep, dumb community with brutes, plants, the rocks, the waters, and one another, as well as our aspiration to something beyond. Music expresses what we feel in the face of nature and of heaven, what we cannot tell when we look into the eyes of animal or man—the unverbalized part of us which feels like the whole of us and is surely the heart of us.

Chapter Eight

DANCING

DALCROZE believes that musical appreciation is best developed by dancing. He regards the body as the perfect musical instrument, and says that one should learn to interpret the slow movements of music with the heavy parts of the body, quick movements with the fingers.[1] One can understand this who has watched the fingers of Kreutzberg. It might be good if people were not required to sit still while listening to a concert, if each person could have a darkened box to himself, free of chairs, in which to move about, kneel or lie down, and freely respond to the music.[2] Dalcroze adds that a plastic response is not necessary to the most profound music because in the deepest emotion

[1] Cf. Jacques-Dalcroze, Emile, *Rhythm, Music, and Education.*
[2] This suggestion comes from a musical friend, Elena Landázuri.

the whole body is innervated in a tension that movement would disturb. But complete immobility is an important part of dancing.

In the dance, as in the movies and the theater, the values of effort and rest, which are fundamental to life, are embodied in human form, where they can be seen and felt as well as heard through music. The appreciation of much modern music which is still unfamiliar, notably that of Stravinsky, is facilitated by presentation with a ballet. Perhaps we profit more from our own efforts at dancing than we can from watching the best dancers. Being spectators at exhibitions of excellence is likely to make us impatient with our own attempts; but the revival of folk-dancing and the continuance of ballroom dancing show that the dance is the heritage of the many as well as the privilege of a few.

Some think of the dance as the supreme art, like Havelock Ellis, who took the idea from Nietzsche, who got it from watching a slack-wire performer. Dancing is living and moving sculpture in which the artist takes his own body, instead of bronze or marble, and makes it assume the ideal forms of beauty. He overcomes awkwardness in himself instead of creating something graceful outside himself. As the musician pours his spirit into his instrument, the dancer insinuates his mind throughout his body. Instead of residing chiefly in his head he moves about in the other regions of his frame, like a friendly monarch among his subjects, becoming one with them and winning them to him, until he is as much at home in his feet as in his head. His members are not just his flesh and blood, but part of his personality. Different moods, which for the rest of us are mostly attitudes of mind unless we can exteriorize them in some substance foreign to ourselves, the dancer embodies in his own body. In him more clearly than elsewhere the spirit becomes incarnate. All his thoughts can be carried out, because he need not carry them outside himself. He is at once the artist and the work of art.

Like each of the fine arts in turn, dancing takes up other arts into itself. It is music, acting, sculpture, and painting. It gets many of the effects of the color organ or clavilux. It combines abstract with human form and amazes man with the beauty of man. Dancing makes us proud of our bodies, enabling us to overcome our sense of physical inferiority to the animals by showing that we can be as supple and sinuous as they, and even surpass them in grace.

Dancing also brings close to us the beauty of nature. Isadora Duncan said: "These flowers before me contain the dream of a dance; it could be named: 'The light falling on white flowers.' A dance that would be a subtle translation of the light and whiteness—so pure, so strong, that people would say, 'It is a soul we see moving, a soul that has reached the light and found the whiteness. We are glad it should move so.' Through its human medium we have a satisfying sense of the movement of light and glad things. Through this human medium, the movement of all nature runs also through us, is transmitted to us from the dancer. We feel the movement of light intermingled with the thought of whiteness. It is a prayer, this dance; each movement reaches in long undulations to the heavens and becomes a part of the eternal rhythm of the spheres."[1]

Isadora Duncan revolted from the fixed forms of the ballet, wishing her dancing to be spontaneous and inspirational. The ballet had become too formal to be expressive, and a revolt was necessary. But there is now a reaction against the vague, subjective dancing of Isadora Duncan's followers, which lacks the balance and design that she instinctively gave to her own performance. Now it is realized that the soul of dancing, which Isadora emphasized, needs the definite structure that the ballet teaches. Technical virtuosity is not necessarily an empty thing; its mechanism may be the means of expressing all sorts of ideas, including the most romantic. It is also important to make a scientific analysis of technique into forms that can be imparted to others. Choreography must be revived and developed so that the pattern of an intricate dance may be put down in notation as convenient as that of music.

The new dancing is more dynamic than the bal-

[1] Kinney, Troy and Margaret West, *The Dance*, pp. 243-244.

109

let, stressing movement rather than the position of the body—the conquest and arrangement of space, rather than a string of poses.[1] But the new dancing will be as formal in design as the ballet, because in dancing as in all art the content must have form. There cannot be freedom without control. There cannot be ends without means. There cannot be beauty without art. Gurney has expressed this in a passage that can be applied to dancing: "In analyzing the delight we derive from the singing . . . of a person whose nature is vividly interesting to us, we shall find, I think, that it is partly due to a perception of the voluntary subjection of freedom and spontaneity to law, of the singer's obedience to a definite order of presentation imagined and set forth by the genius of another. Somewhat as the essential force of words gains instead of losing by its restraint within the forms of meter, so all independent individuality seems to gain piquancy from the sense that in one direction its possessor is self-controlled into being the

[1] Cf. Denby, Edwin, "Art and Craft in Dancing," *Theatre Guild Magazine*, January, 1929; and Martin, John, "The Dance Is Attuned to the Machine," *New York Times Magazine*, February 24, 1929.

110

medium and channel of an ordered beauty existing outside the personality of this or that performer, and appealing on its inherent merits to the emotions of the listeners."[1]

The importance of bodily discipline in the beauty of the dance is symbolic of the place that control of the body should have in life. Mr. F. Matthias Alexander has pointed out[2] that habit has become inadequate to the control of the body's muscles, in view of the new demands of civilization. He says that only by becoming fully conscious of our bodies can we recover the harmonious functioning that is natural to animals. He believes that by achieving conscious control of our bodies we can adapt ourselves even to the most civilized life without any loss of well-being. By learning to economize effort we may become as frictionless in all our actions as a dancer.

Primitive peoples all center their lives in dancing, and the most civilized have most honored the dance. We ourselves appreciate what is essentially

[1] Gurney, Edmund, *The Power of Sound*, p. 475.
[2] Cf. *Man's Supreme Inheritance*.

111

dancing in our admiration of the skill that we happen to understand. We know that in handling trunks the knack of it is more important than size or strength. We know that a little man who knows how can outbox, outrun, or outdrive a big man who does not know how. We are aware that in any sport an athlete's "form" is more important than his build. We admire acrobats whole-heartedly, and enjoy the dancing of softshoe artists and skaters. A musical comedy or a débutante cannot succeed without dancing. Dancers are necessary in an opera company, and we are beginning to appreciate dancing as an independent art as important as any other.

Castiglione says in his *Book of the Courtier*, the etiquette book of the Renaissance, that one should "practice in everything a certain nonchalance that shall conceal design and show that what is done and said is done without effort and almost without thought. From this I believe grace is in large measure derived, because everyone knows the difficulty of those things that are rare and well done, and therefore facility in them excites the highest admiration; while, on the other hand, to strive and, as the saying is, to drag by the hair, is extremely ungraceful, and makes us esteem everything slightly, however great it may be."[1]

We come away from a football game so impressed with the apparent ease of strenuous effort and so full of kinæsthetic sensations of running and dodging, that it is hard to refrain from dashing through the crowd as if carrying the ball in a game of our own. We leave a boxing-match keyed up for a fight on our own account. We steal away from the zoo with cautious tread, as if tigers and lions were prowling in us. We retain, from watching a ballet, a twinkle in our feet, a ripple in all our muscles, a glow of physical consciousness as if we were no longer pedestrians, but dancers. We move to music, we are controlled by rhythm weaving a colorful web, as if we had left the earth to glide through the sky, diaphanous and filmy, melting and mixing with clouds against the illumination of a sunset.

Through empathy we assume the movements of

[1] Translation of Leonard Opdycke (Scribners), p. 35

the dancer and seem to gain his control over our own bodies, as if we could integrate and flex ourselves with his grace. Since anything which appears in one scale of being can be transposed to another, the lightness and sureness of the dancer may be used to facilitate our spiritual as well as physical carriage, so that we may float through life and spring to our fate like him.

The life of primitive men revolved about the dance. They danced for the hunt, for rain, for war, for love. The dance was central in their religion, being their way of praying. It was the matrix of their drama, story, music, and song. Even the Greek drama began as a dance form, arising as it did from ancient ritual,[1] while Greek sculpture and painting took over and fixed the attitudes and gestures of festival dancers. Perhaps all Greek culture and philosophy were the flowering of the dance.[2] Dancing has had no small part in the ritual of Christianity, though for some time it has been limited to special festivals, unless the mass itself be

[1] Cf. Harrison, Jane, *Ancient Art and Ritual*.
[2] Cf. Clark, Louisa Lewis, *The Dance in Relation to Other Arts* (A master's dissertation at the University of Chicago).

considered a dance. Religion has ever been an effort to get into harmony with the universe, and the universe has long been thought to have a rhythm. It is natural to suppose that the sun and stars dance in the heavens. St. Basil wrote to St. Gregory: "What could be more blessed than to imitate on earth the rhythm of the angels?"[1] The good life consists in imitating the ideal, and compared with the way most of us hitch along, the grace of the dancer is divine. While we are weighed down by our bodies, he makes his own as buoyant as spirit. As if he could not stumble or tire, he walks on air like a god.

To grow more graceful is not only to appear better, but to work better. Labor has always been lightened by emphasis on rhythm, making it easier for the individual to coördinate his own movements and to coöperate with those of others. In fact, it is impossible to accomplish any task without rhythm. Nietzsche regarded his writing as dancing, for even intellectual work must be rhythmical. All purposeful living proceeds through a

[1] Kinney, Troy and Margaret West, *The Dance*, p. 30.

115

series of problems and solutions, involving repeated loss and recovery of balance. Thought has
steps like dance steps. It has groupings of units
like the *enchaînements* of dancing, which may be
formed into a whole like a ballet.

When we live like dancers, our posture at rest
and in action is altered. We become like figures
in a painting or a frieze. We have poise, movement
in repose, and repose in movement. Our mind mirrors our bodily mood, our thoughts turn and twirl,
they sway and bow, they unfold and close like
flowers, they die and come to life like the seasons.
Our minds are dissolved in our bodies, our bodies
are absorbed in a dance. We are reconciled to flesh
become divine, we can believe that the perfect
body is the soul. We can understand the legend of
the Jongleur de Notre Dame—he could not pray
as others did, but he could dance; he danced for
Our Lady, and she was well pleased with his
worship.

Dancing symbolizes the keeping of equilibrium
on the wire of life over the pit of death. All existence is an effort to maintain a balance, compensat-

ing one shift of weight with another, continually tripping and avoiding falling, as gracefully as possible. To live well we must learn to walk, to work, and to play with economy of energy. Our social as well as our physical existence is one of delicate balancing, of prevented false steps and falls. We express this by saying that successful people have poise. In trying situations, when the slack wire of destiny is swaying beneath them, they smile and are unperturbed, as if standing on *terra firma.* The only firm ground is self-possession. Other support is sought in vain.

To live a human life one must stand erect—no mean achievement—and walk about with ease. Many a one who can stand on the physical plane gets dizzy on higher levels, though the trick is the same. An accomplished performer is as sure of himself up close to the ridge-pole as near the earth, and most cool when no net is spread beneath him, because his life depends upon himself. Some people, like Tartarin, trust Providence to put safety nets beneath the most perilous heights. They trust to luck, but luck is never as trustworthy as art. Because they have art, bull-fighters can dance with death, barely avoiding the bull by twirling and swerving their bodies, while they stay in the same place, without fear, without flight, with calm, with skill, with a smile.

The more delicate the adjustments that we have to make, the more value we shall find in the sight of dancers and all who live like dancers. From them we may learn that even mental inertia, like physical gravity, when overcome, will contribute to artistic living; that life may be a graceful balancing of ideas against any odds.

Chapter Nine

ARCHITECTURE

THE need for housing is so fundamental that the most primitive shelter has beauty if it will not cave in or topple over; and man is influenced by the external equilibrium of his buildings much as life is permeated by the internal, personal balancing of the dance. If it is reasonable to believe that the five or more races of man owe their characteristics to geographical distribution, to the sky above them, the soil beneath them, and the air they breathe; architecture, which immediately spans humanity, must profoundly affect it. Though the nature of construction is largely dictated by the character of the region in which it is undertaken, his edifices are the most unavoidable part of man's fate, the most inescapable coil of his environment. Buildings are his life and its limitation; they allow

119

him to look out and they shut him in. They are his walls and his windows.

In architecture man lives and moves and has his being. He is born indoors. He makes love, gets married, and dies in the house. He learns his lessons, earns his living, takes his rest, and has half his fun inside. His home is a house, his school is a schoolhouse, his club a clubhouse, his business a business house, and his church a God's house. Each of his interests is housed. His government, education, religion, and all his institutions are most readily thought of as buildings.

When we imagine a civilization or epoch in history we usually visualize its architecture. The most monumental feature of a period is its buildings, and in them we naturally locate its other attributes. In thinking of an individual man we remember his outward lineaments, because they are most obvious and because we regard them as expressive of his personality. Similarly, in thinking of a people we call to mind their external aspect, because it is conspicuous and believed to be characteristic. The Sphinx, the Pyramids, and the tremendous temples by the Nile are the awe of time that was Egypt. The Parthenon is the symmetry and serenity that was Greece. The Coliseum, the Forum, the aqueducts arching across the Campagna, the roads and bridges of the Romans, and all the far-flung ruins of the Empire, are the grandeur that was Rome. Taj Mahal is the luxury of the East. The cathedrals and manors of Europe are the Middle Ages. Palaces of Florence are the Renaissance. Factories and tenements of Manchester, Birmingham, and Leeds are the Industrial Revolution. The caravels of Columbus, the *Mayflower*, the log cabin and the covered wagon are the New World. Steamships in the harbor of New York, its roaring streets and recessional skyscrapers, the railroads, office buildings and hotels of Chicago, are the Twentieth Century.

As we move among the rooms of a house, or go about the streets of a city, we also walk down the aisles of the past, wander in the transepts of the present, and peer up to the dim arches of the future. Ever the plan of the mind is altered by the place that it alters, as if the mind were amorphous

and had no structure of its own, or as if its residence had no fixed form, but took on the architecture of the mind. A person is often so reticent
in speech and cautious in conduct that it is difficult
to judge his character unless we have an opportunity to visit his home town where we can stroll
about the streets and alleys of his mind, breathe
the weather of his moods, enter the home of his
soul, and go from room to room of his personality. After that there may be details of his self
that we do not know, but the nature of it is clear,
because what a man cannot mold in his environment, it will mold in him. If he cannot perceptibly
change his town, he can paint and furnish his
house; if he cannot even do that, at least he can
affect his own room in the house. The degree of
his failure to impress himself upon his surround-
ings indicates the extent of their impression on
him, for he and they will fit like hand and glove,
like shoe and foot; where one will not give, the
other must.

While perhaps architecture has been the fine art
least appreciated by us, we are beginning to see

that it overarches all. Only upon occasion do we
go to hear music, take time to visit galleries of
painting and sculpture, or have an opportunity to
really read, but whatever we are doing or not
doing, we constantly live in the presence of architecture. Whether we are working, playing, waking,
or sleeping, it is always there, silently making us
what we are. We cannot be the same now, in our
separate, cell-like rooms as people whose home
life was spent about the fireplace in a common
living-room. Santa Fé adobe houses in which one
room leads into another through doorways without doors, all on the same plan, seem to make access from one soul to another easier than in east-
ern houses, where a person alone in his room is
cut off from other people. The Reformation, with
its sense of sin and individual responsibility, may
have appeared in northern Europe because there
people were more shut in than in the south, and
more likely to brood.

Every phase of life may be affected by architecture. The psychical and perhaps the chemical
effects of eating in a cafeteria are not the same as

those of eating in a club or a home. Sleep has a different quality on a train, in a tent, and in a castle. For beings who sleep differently in various houses, and in different rooms of the same house, the cause of insomnia or of freedom from it may be architecture. The bed itself is important, but it is easier to fit the body than the mind, and the mind does not sleep so much in a bed as in a bedroom. Roses on the wall may disturb the psyche more than the petal under the mattress worried the princess.

The spirit identifies itself with its carnal integument and receives experience through the senses of the body. In turn the body is the soul of the buildings in which it is embodied, taking over and contributing to their strength or weakness, delicacy or candor. A mind could not be the same in the physique of Emile Zola as in that of Marcel Proust, as it could hardly maintain the same quality in the Bastille as in La Sainte Chapelle. Nor could a body or a building remain uninfluenced by the spirit of its tenant. Everyone has a different feeling in a church from what one has in a club. This is

not hypocrisy, it is not even strange, it is architecture. It is like the change in atmosphere between London, Paris, and Vienna. Architecture is
much of the difference between Londoners, Pari-
sians, and the Viennese.

The comparative neglect of architecture in the
United States has been equally indicative of American life. The spirit of pioneers, opening up a new
country, could not have built the kind of structure
that requires stability, a resting in one place
through an unhurried present, with the sense of a
past in the same place, and a future that will be
there also. The frontier theory of architecture was
a cabin for the time being, and a covered wagon
in which to move on. In our day the cabin is the
efficiency apartment, the covered wagon is the
Pullman and the automobile.

There is beauty in any satisfaction, but we are
beginning to feel dissatisfied with what is merely
relief from physical discomfort. Because we now
wish to move elegantly as well as smoothly and
swiftly, and because we now ride for the joy of it
as much as to be going somewhere, conveyances

are being designed with more subtlety. Here is a kind of architecture that we all appreciate, being familiar with its problems and purposes. People are naturally particular about their vehicles when they enjoy them perhaps more than they do their homes. The automobile architects of different companies vie in a rivalry that becomes increasingly artistic as their customers become harder to please. Though an efficient engine is æsthetic as well as good lines, the success of an automobile depends largely on its looks, because when essentials have been taken care of, improvement must be in accessories. Even filling stations, when they perform their main function equally well, compete on their appearance.

At home, as in travel, we are no longer at ease with physical comfort if we must do without the charm that we are coming to expect of architecture. A chair cannot satisfy that is merely to sit on. All furniture should have double usefulness, serving immediate and remoter needs, delighting sight and touch in addition to being convenient. The outside of a house should do more than cover the inside; the interior should be more than a retreat from the weather. Besides rooms for eating, sleeping, and the necessities, the same rooms or others ought to be appropriate for luxuries like conversation and reverie, in a house that would be a home.

Since any value is beautiful in contemplation, beauty is not only added grace, gratuitous flourish. A crust of bread is æsthetic to the hungry, a drink of water to the thirsty. Loveliness feeds on the plain fare of satisfaction. But when refinement is pleasing, then it also answers to need and may be needed enough to be necessary. Trifling though it seem, it may be what Voltaire calls a tremendous trifle. In the architecture of a supremely beautiful building, more than the main demand is fulfilled. The best house is one in which living is above bare existence; the best factory is one in which work is more than employment. Most often as a church, however, has an edifice been erected that seems to meet every wish, treating each requirement as lovingly as the chief desire. To make every inch significant is to manifest divine sympathy with every bit of human longing.

When a man contemplates a cathedral he follows a mystic plan through a thousand variations, turning and returning on itself, flowing over the floor, welling up the arches to the shadowy vaulting, swirling about the rose window, streaming through the clerestory windows; shifting and transposing from volume and mass to design, to line, to color, to symbol; reiterating itself in the frescoes, in the stained glass, in the images in the niches; mimicking and iterating itself in the gargoyles, in the fish, fowl, and beasts of fable, and all the incidents of Scripture, carved on the doors and formed in the mosaics; reverberating in the roll and tremble of the organ; echoing in the chant of the celebrants of the mass; representing and repeating itself in the mystery and spell of that ceremony, in the vestments, the candles, the incense—until a man feels multiplied by manifoldness and summed up in oneness.

Sometimes an actual structure so exalts the spectator that its beauty is transcendent. Such a time was that of the illumination of St. Peter's in Rome after the canonization of St. Theresa of Lisieux. The lighting was achieved in part by electricity, but largely by candles. Seen from a distant balcony, except for stars, the Aurora Borealis, and sunsets, there never had been a vision more splendid. The outlines of the cathedral were alive with fire. One realized its magnitude more than in the daytime, when one could not help thinking that some of it must be buildings around it. That night it was all a luminous unity. The façade extended forward like a celestial rampart shining in the darkness. Far back, two cupolas rose against the sky, while between and behind and above them, over all, leaped in shimmering undulations the big dome, capped by its lantern, surmounted by a cross of light. Long one watched, when of a sudden a flame spread over the whole. Then not only the lines but the surfaces of the entire edifice were incandescent. There were crosses and patterns of crosses that glowed and flickered in the wind. No longer was there a solid building resting on the ground, but a resplendent miracle that might float off among the constellations.

But wonderful as a single building can be, a greater architectural achievement is a beautiful city. The beauty of private dwellings is of small importance compared with the value of noble public structures, handsome streets, and parks that may be enjoyed by all. Since human beings are sensitive to their environment, it ought to be conducive throughout to the best life. Nothing is more civilizing and humanizing than a city planned to meet all the needs of its citizens.

Towns were first fortified against military attack, then against famine and disease. To our shame there still remain slums breeding tuberculosis and crime and lesser evils, which might be mitigated by city planning. Zoning laws keep residence districts free from trade. Streets are widened, straightened, or curved to make it pleasant to be going as well as to arrive somewhere. Green parkways and trees come to be valued as much as thoroughfares themselves. In many cities the waterfront, which has been an eyesore, is being allowed to have its proper attraction. In Chicago, boulevards are laid out along the river in place of the jumble of docks, warehouses, and markets that were there; and a drive is built along Lake Michigan, on land filled in beyond the railroad tracks that formerly spoiled the shore.

Unplanned urban districts, and whole cities that were hardly planned at all, are often beautiful by accident, by association, and by sentiment. But adventitious beauty cannot be accorded a high place in architecture or any art. Real art is an integration of means and ends, with results that are sought and intended by men who know what they are about. If a building or a city happens to have charm for us because we spent our childhood in it, or because a loved one lived there, this has nothing to do with its architecture. If we are able to imagine significance that builders had not achieved, we can compose a work of literary art out of the elements before us. Literary value can be discovered in the most haphazard building, or in ruins.

But no romancing is necessary to the appreciation of a structure that clearly satisfies the needs for which it was designed.

In famous cities of the past, however handsomely a few needs were provided for, many wants of the inhabitants were miserably neglected. In the future all the requirements of an entire city will be anticipated as far as possible by architects. Then architectural beauty will not be limited to a few places that men enter only occasionally, alcoves off from the reality of living.

People live in cities more than in homes, because the most complete home can house only part of a modern life. One must rely upon civic organization for livelihood, for food, sanitation, and safety, as private control of these things is vanishing. If homes are not self-sufficient in physical affairs, they are less so in intellectual and social matters. It is no longer feasible to carry on the whole of education privately. Religion never was altogether private. The truth is that human beings have almost always lived gregariously, in clans, tribes, and villages of one sort or another. Even in a metropolis neighborhoods and clubs form to prevent isolation. People want some privacy, but not too much. They want their own homes—in a community where they can do without their own cows and wells. They want to live their own lives, but do not want to do all their own washing, sewing, cooking, and baking. By pooling their needs they are able to save time, expense, and bother in satisfying them. People are beginning to see that keeping up separate roofs and furnaces is needlessly extravagant. By putting their houses together in a common building they can get rid of many responsibilities and expenses.

The trouble with big buildings heretofore is that they have been foisted on towns that were not planned for them. A city designed for skyscrapers would combine the advantages of solitude and society. It would relieve traffic instead of congesting it, because most of the travel would be up and down in elevators. Each edifice might be a town in itself, with one roof and one basement, but with many homes, comfortable, light, and airy, and enough shops to supply their wants.[1]

Later a nation might be designed as architecturally as a city, and finally the whole world. Then everywhere the good things of the open country might accompany those of associated living. The Garden City of Ebenezer Howard's dream would be more than realized, and perhaps the New Jerusalem of John's vision, supremely beautiful in achieving all the values of human life.

[1] Cf. Walker, Ralph Thomas, "The Relation of Skyscrapers to Our Life," condensed in the Reader's Digest, July, 1930, from The Architectural Forum, May, 1930.

Chapter Ten

LITERATURE

THOUGH architecture is yet building the New Jerusalem, that city has long since been described in literature. Through literary art even our present towns are transformed into celestial cities. When Blake said that the cottages about him were shadows of the angels' houses, their architecture did not matter. Literature does not simply accept the familiar aspect of things, but makes us aware of the mysterious background of experience. The vast setting, in which great books make us at home, may excite and comfort us so much that we may love to be alone with them, with nothing before us but solitude and silence.

Literary values are simply human values expressed in words. The function of literature is not different from that of other arts, though it has

135

characteristics of its own. The verbal art, like any art, tries to objectify what men value, to furnish what they wish. But rather than have its message relayed by the senses, literature endeavors to talk tête-à-tête with the mind, trying to tell what can scarcely be told, yet must be said. Because it must speak the ineffable, literature is the most difficult and defeated of the arts.[1] Occasionally it penetrates to the soul and whispers a word that ruffles the silence, breathes a wingèd word, flying from mind to mind, a word which is more than the moving of lips, more than the sound of a voice, an articulate word, which says what it means; that is magic.

Perhaps we can never know when an author has succeeded in telling us what he had intended. We have no sufficient ground for supposing that we derive from the writings of the Greeks what they put into them. We must interpret words in terms of our experience, and in so far as our experience is unique our understanding must be peculiar. Even when we learn to read the original Greek,

---

[1] *"La parole humaine est comme un chaudron fêlé où nous battons des mélodies à faire danser les ours, quand on voudrait attendrir les étoiles."*—Flaubert, Gustave, *Madame Bovary*, p. 212.

it is likely that we merely learn another notation for our own notions, instead of grasping the ideas of the Greeks. Anatole France says: "I do not hesitate to say that at the present time we do not understand a single verse of *The Iliad* or *The Divine Comedy* in the sense that was initially attached to it. To live is to change, and the posthumous life of our written thoughts is not released from this law; they will not continue to exist except on the condition of becoming more and more different from that which they were upon issuing from our mind. That which will be admired in us in the future will become altogether strange to us."[1]

Philologists say that no two people ever use words in quite the same way, that two persons never pronounce the same word in the same way, and that it is impossible for the same man to pronounce a word twice in precisely the same way. Since each word permits of any number of intonations and shades of meaning, it is nearly impossible, when hearing a word, let alone when reading it, to seize its exact significance. In a phrase of two

[1] *Les Opinions de M. Jérôme Coignard*, pp. 6, 7.

words the possible meanings amount to the square of infinity.

While the comprehension of words is inherently so difficult, the multiplication and dissemination of words by various agencies does not diminish vagueness. People exclaim at the wonder of words being communicated thousands of miles through the ether, but words have to traverse a tremendous distance to come from a speaker in the same room. When lips brush against an ear, what they whisper may not be plain. Yet a man will hope, by means of words, to speak from the bottom of his aloneness to the aloneness of another.

Ordinarily we appear able to say fairly well what we mean and to be understood, because in conversation words are heard in the light of the situation in which they are uttered. They are clarified by vocal inflexion, and by facial and bodily gesture. On paper the same words might mean very little, or they might mean as much as they would in colloquy, and still, from the literary point of view, mean nothing. Literature must mean more than conversation ordinarily signifies, or it is insignificant. It is because commonly we do not mean anything particular that we are able to say pretty much what we mean. We speak carelessly, striking in the midst of several meanings, whenever we are able to understand one another without being exact. When distinctions are not valued and precision is not sought, we are not disturbed by the indefiniteness of what is said. But in literature, as Conrad says, "it is only through an unremitting never-discouraged care of the shape and ring of sentences that an approach can be made to plasticity, to colour; and the light of magic suggestiveness may be brought to play for an evanescent instant over the commonplace surface of words: of the old, old words, worn thin, defaced by ages of careless usage."[1]

If literature does not use words more nicely than the world employs them, it is not literature; and if it does, the world may not appreciate it, but literature must have value that can be appreciated by the world. A writer must be original without being incomprehensible, and plain without being dull.

[1] Conrad, Joseph, Preface to *The Nigger of the Narcissus.*

139

He must have fresh insight, and he must correlate it with the commonplace. He must bring heaven down and earth up. He must combine uniqueness with universality. Since people cannot learn what they have not already begun to learn, and take little interest in what they have mastered, a writer must be very skillful neither to mystify nor to bore his readers. He must say what they can see, but would not have seen had he not said it. He must reveal them to themselves, showing them that they are wiser than they knew. This is the most exciting experience that readers can have: to come across something strange and wonderful, yet to feel that they have known it all the time, though they had been unable to express it. Readers can never be grateful enough to the writer who can give them this. When they have found him they have found themselves. Then they cannot live without him; they keep him by their pillows, carry him in their pockets, and treasure him in their hearts, for he is more themselves than they are.

A writer is most powerful when he can express himself in terms of what is already believed, and at-the same time awaken a fuller perception of the possibilities in life. The beauty of literature is that it can show men the ideal and help them toward it. Great literature proves that the ideal is to become more human by achieving deeper love and better understanding. Lovers of literature know that to contemplate the world whole-heartedly and to move in it imaginatively is to find nothing utterly inhuman, in the sense of being hopelessly unlovely or incomprehensible. Literature is writing that makes men alive to values where they had known ugliness or banality.

Literature not only builds fictions that satisfy the heart, but brings out values in life that are not fictitious. A made-up story is not interesting to a mature mind unless it rests upon probability; though a plausible narrative is uninteresting, no matter how well authenticated with facts, unless it is somehow startling. Literature must come home both to what men know and to what they feel. It is always human and never detached from actual experience, as George Moore would have us believe in his *Anthology of Pure Poetry.* Every poem

that he has admitted to his collection defies his
definition of pure art as a vision apart from the
personality of the poet, concerned entirely with
objective things, and having nothing to do with
ideas or human reactions. If such a poetry of things
in themselves were possible, it would be inhuman.
The songs of Shakespeare, in which Mr. Moore
delights, are not descriptions of a noumenal world,
but of human emotions, which things evoke and
symbolize. Autolycus urges lads to buy of him lest
their lasses cry, though he does name the things
that maids lack from head to heel. In Desdemona's
song there are no things that do not present themselves to her as ideas full of emotion. The fresh
streams and the softened stones would not matter
in themselves. Mr. Moore tries to rule out all poetry with a taint of subjectivity, and then quotes
a song with a capital "I" in nearly every line:

> Where the bee sucks, there suck I:
> In a cowslip's bell I lie;
> There I couch when owls do cry.
> On the bat's back I do fly
> After summer merrily.

142

Merrily, merrily shall I live now
Under the blossom that hangs on the bough.

In this self-conscious age when personality is highly prized, literary art must be important, since it stresses personal values. A self develops under the influence of other selves, but only a fraction of the contacts that are craved can be found in actual intercourse. In literature the personality can be excited, exercised, and quieted as much as desired. In literature a recluse may know all kinds of people, and a person tired of society can find sympathy. In books various lives can be lived vicariously, and the difficulties of reality can be forgotten or discounted.

Literary art, however, is not valued merely as an escape or a fortress. There are delicate, tender books that are clung to through everything. Some of the most beautiful books seem sad and disheartening, but are somehow comforting. Literature cannot be limited to cheery volumes; it must include all the writing that men cherish. Protection and encouragement are not the only vital human needs. The upper lip needs stiffening, but the tear-ducts

143

and the risibles need exercise as well. A book that makes one laugh and cry, and brace up, too, has triple worth.

Rather than narrow too much the list of books that are literary, it were better to say that any book which is read belongs to literature. A man does not continue to read what has no value for him. Every man is free to get what he may from any books he chooses, and cannot be forced to find in famous works what is not there for him. *The Magic Mountain* by Thomas Mann is exciting to one person and depressing to another. A book is not the right one for a man whom it cripples and dismays, any more than stories like *Tom Thumb* and *Hansel and Gretel* are good for a child whom they frighten. To be worth while a book must facilitate adjustment in life and contribute to happiness. There are different conceptions of happiness and success, but books that stir people to live more vividly or steady them to live more serenely are always valued.

Literary books are those that give æsthetic experience; that involve contemplation of something

144

beyond, that make one stand on tiptoe to reach a higher self. A book that does not demand any mental and emotional effort is not literature; though some literary masterpieces are so ingratiating that the effort required to read them is not resented or even noticed, except as agreeably stimulating. A book too difficult to be appreciated is not art; nor is one too easy to be interesting. What is literature for one reader may not be for another, but when one derives æsthetic experience from a book, one is in the presence of literature. A book that excites the desire for something more in life, and at the same time satisfies that desire, is a work of art. Some readers are harder to excite and soothe than others; but writers with a public easy to please receive praise that makes them seem greater than authors with a fastidious following.

Everyone is free to make up a list of classics. Literature, like life, is wide open. There is no exclusive way to write any more than there is only one way to live. Any mode of existence is life, whether we ourselves like it or not; and any book that makes life more livable for some one is litera-

145

ture for that one, regardless of the pundits. Rules of grammar and rhetoric attempt to show how books that are read were written; but as soon as enough people read books otherwise written, the grammarians and rhetoricians must get busy again or be ignored. Though thousands turn up their noses at the movies, they are art to millions, and so are the popular books that the *literati* will not read.

Despite the relativity of taste, however, it is impossible to refrain from setting up standards. They may simply be indications of what happens to be liked, but in art and life a preference is a standard. No one reads a book without liking or disliking it, and comparing it with other books as better, worse, or equal in value. A boy who is entranced with dime novels of the *Pluck and Luck* variety, or detective stories of the Nick Carter kind, is having æsthetic experience as long as he genuinely enjoys them. The boy could not be absorbed in pages that were trash to him. When he buys cheap magazines of romance and adventure he is feeding an urge that may become an aspiration; and, however mild his thrills may be beside those of one who reads Euripides in Greek, many an epicure of exquisite prose might envy his delight. A boy rightly abides by what enriches life for him until he finds something more nourishing, perhaps in the vivacity of Dumas and the virility of Jack London. But blood and thunder will turn to milk and water when he is dazzled by the leashed lightning in psychology. Then he will lose interest in violent action, and relish the subtleties of Proust more than the suspense of *The Moonstone.*

One can show that a writer is great by reading him with devotion and winning others to him. Enthusiasm is contagious, and nothing so recommends an author as a discriminating person's attachment to him. One who is well acquainted with books can guide the reading of other people by saying that if they like this book they ought to like that one; that if they do not care for this they will scarcely value that. With the help of such hints a man can go from old favorites to new ones, and avoid books that are uncongenial. Thus taste is formed. Writers acclaimed by authors whom we already love usually have value for us, and they in turn will introduce us to other kindred spirits. Anatole France alone could supply his admirers with a list of books for a lifetime, each of them guaranteed by his personality to be good as long as he is good. If and when his appeal is no longer valid for us we shall have discovered new guides whom we can trust to name the best books for us.

We should be glad that some of them we cannot touch for a long while, because it is most exciting to finally open a book whose title has enticed us for years. It is not immoral to glance into books that we do not finish, and often it is more profitable to browse in many books than to read a few from cover to cover. If we ever exhaust our reading list, instead of complaining that there is nothing more to read, we can be thankful for leisure to think over what we have perused, and know the luxury of beginning again the books that we love.

We need not regret our earlier taste, because if once we liked Edgar Guest we were on the way to like Byron more and Dante still more. The most vital experience is that of growth, and for many people there is no better way to develop and to realize progress than in advancing from reading of lesser value to literature that is the pinnacle of life. We may go from *Treasure Island* to *Lord Jim*; from *Little Women* to *Pride and Prejudice*; from the *Essays of Elia* to the dialogues of Plato and the matchless English of Santayana. We may vault the inhibitions that often screen the humanity of famous books, and become as familiar with Chaucer and the Bible as children should be with *Mother Goose* and *Little Black Sambo*.

We need to distinguish between prose and poetry no more than children do who are equally entranced with fairy tales and nursery rhymes, noticing no more difference between them than wise men can discover, who point out that good poetry, despite its formality, is as flexible as prose; that good prose, for all its freedom, is reined in by a hidden rhythm as compelling as that of poetry. No one can chart the deviations that are the charm of Shakespeare and Milton. No one can explain the mechanism by which are delicately controlled the

149

majestic sentences of Ruskin and the fiery passages of Nietzsche.

It seems a far cry from fiction to philosophy, but the value of the novel is the wisdom it gives for the conduct and enjoyment of life; while the good of philosophy is the tale of the mind's adventures and the story of affairs that most concern the heart. All writing that helps men to be more human, more wise and kind, is literature. The writings of Kant and Spinoza belong to literature because they foster gentleness and intelligence.

The works of William James and John Dewey, because they also are supremely humanizing, are perhaps the greatest books in American literature. They not only edify but vitalize. They are bracing and refreshing. They take life at its lowest terms and find value; they take life at its best and see room for improvement. If existence must be idealized before we can like it, there is danger of disillusion; and if living cannot be ameliorated there is danger of discouragement. When we can love life on the level, like James and Dewey, we should neither be puffed up nor cast down. Something like the coarseness of Zola and the innocence of Keats are necessary to acceptance of the universe; and a Rabelaisian sense of humor that can filter clean fun from dirt that horrifies the squeamish. The great yea-sayers find beauty in the most unlikely places and put it in their books where we can see it when we cannot find it elsewhere.

When all other arts fail, literature comes to the rescue. It reveals beauty in buildings that architecturally are hopeless, in noise that could never be music, and in scenes that defy painting. Literature salvages what other arts cannot redeem, and glorifies it. In literature the ruins of art and life are made appealing. Sickness and disaster are turned inside out by words and woven into happiness. Words are the bravest defense man has, the Swiss Guard of the spirit. Other defenders quail before the worst, unless supported by words that give comfort and courage even in the face of death.

Chapter Eleven

PRINTING

THE literature of Greece and the Middle Ages might have perished but for the patience of copyists whose manuscripts, beautifully written and often illuminated, are treasured today as a lost art. The only call for calligraphy now is in the making of diplomas and the engrossing of rare presentation volumes. Penmanship has been superseded by printing as the art of preserving all the arts. The best examples of handwriting itself are perpetuated in type designed after them, as well as in photographic prints of the original. Even Egyptian inscriptions are printed on paper to be read when the Pyramids have crumbled.

Literature, as we know it, would be impossible without printing. The composition of music would be hampered without the dissemination of musical notation by means of the press. Works of painting, sculpture, and architecture would be comparatively still-born if known only in the original and not in countless printed reproductions. The theater, the movies, and the dance might get along without printing, but hardly their history, criticism, and advertisement. Not only the fine arts, but all the arts of living would be crippled without the mani-folding and preserving of their lore through print-ing. In business and science, in philosophy and religion, in love and education, in any art of life that should be aware of the finest values and able to attain them, the art of printing is indispensable.

Because multitudes find the highest values in the Bible, it continues to be the most printed book in the world. This may help to explain the magical persuasiveness of printing. The printed pages most familiar to people have been those of their holy book, and they have been prone to accept anything in type as gospel truth. The time is not remote when a charlatan, trying to hypnotize a crowd into buying a new-fangled remedy, could rely upon the distribution of his claims in print to vouch for their veracity. Even sophisticated folk are likely to have more respect for ideas after they have been printed than while they are still in manuscript, however clearly written or typewritten.

The best typewriting looks home made and tentative compared with the finish and finality of print. The margin of a printed page is even on the right side as well as on the left, and the spacing to make the lines come out the same is done imperceptibly. Seldom are there mistakes in spelling, and the typographical errors which inevitably occur are rarely discovered by an eye not practiced in their detection. The standardization of style brought about by printers, the uniformity and accuracy of their work, all give dignity and distance to what they publish.

When ideas have been set up and run off on the press they acquire a permanence and impersonality that it seems must belong to wisdom. Once they have been stamped with immortality by the press, to go echoing down the ages, it is hard to realize that all printed thoughts have not come from an oracular origin; that some of them are only the opinions of fellow-citizens who have not got over the thrill of being printed. That thrill is so real that even a seasoned author will turn to his own article in a journal and perhaps read it over without glancing at the other contributions. A reporter has lost interest in life who does not look for his own stuff first in the paper. Merely to have one's name appear in print is glamorous, because that is the way famous names usually appear. Most well-known personalities have left their bodies to survive in the letters of their names, so that to get into print is to live on like David and Solomon, and Jeroboam, the son of Nebat, who made Israel to sin.

Three minutes after an event has occurred it can be printed in a newspaper as it might be read a thousand years later, and precisely as if it had taken place a millennium ago, irrevocably shoved over the deadline into the past. Reams of paper, the pulp of forests, are fed into rotary presses to emerge covered with words. It is fascinating to see a painting slowly form on canvas, but presswork is instantaneous. Where there was blankness a moment before, now there are lines and columns of words, as if they had always been there. They are not all trustworthy, but to one who knows how to read them they are reasonably veracious, and more easily credited than Scripture.

Printing so fills our lives that moments not occupied with reading are only the margins of our time. The margins are wider with some than with others, but scarcely anyone has days devoid of print, considering the advertisements and directions that crowd the interstices of existence. Persons who have no other literary taste pore over tickers, menus, and programs. People who have no libraries may not escape form letters, invitations, and calling-cards. Even folk who devote their leisure to bridge have minds well inked with printed symbols. Playing-cards are among the finest triumphs of printing, and the demand for them was conducive to the improvement of printing that facilitated the spread of knowledge upon which rests our civilization.

The value of printing is so great that it is natural to lovingly embellish it; but for its value to be widely available its cost must be moderate. From the time of what is regarded as the beginning of printing, in the fifteenth century, it has been a question whether the making of books should be an expensive art for the few or a cheap art for the many. The very invention of printing implies that to popularize books is better than keeping them costly and inaccessible. To publish means to make public. But the exquisite work of scribes was the model for early printers, and they were uncomfortably aware of the difference between a glittering manuscript and a printed book.

When printing came to be recognized as a fine art in its own right, Firmin Didot placed the royal printing-office of France on the same basis as the institutions of Gobelins and Sèvres, and was decorated for his artistry with the ribbon of the Legion of Honor.[1] Printing became such a fashionable accomplishment that kings of France and their mistresses amused themselves with presses of their own.[2] To this day only connoisseurs appreciate or

[1] Cf. Putnam, George Haven, *Books and Their Makers During the Middle Ages,* p. 191.
[2] Cf. Oswald, John Clyde, *A History of Printing,* p. 265.

pay for the finest printing. People who care chiefly for the contents of a book would not try to own the princely volumes of Bodoni, because they would not prize his fine typography, skillful press-work and lavish use of rare paper.[1] People who think that a book is primarily to be read would not buy the Kelmscott *Chaucer*, because it is nearly un-readable. William Morris, who printed it, ab-horred blank space as much as Bodoni loved it, though formality in printing was equally close to his heart. Morris designed type faces to occupy the entire body; he used little or no leading between the lines, and did all that he could to mass the blackness on a page, even recasting sentences in his own writings to fill out the lines.[2] In such printing, as well as in bindings sumptuously tooled, studded with jewels, or covered with satin and embroidered with wool, the guiding motive is the look and feel of a book regardless of readability. Luxurious bookmaking may harmonize with an author's words and enhance them, as at the Doves Bindery,

[1] *Ibid.*, p. 252.
[2] Cf. Orcutt, William Dana, *Master Makers of the Book*, p. 218.

where each binding is designed for a particular book. But most printers have had to choose between catering to those who value the sensuous externals of a book, and pleasing the scholar whose desire is for the text itself. Fancy printers strive to avoid the commonplace in curious ways that are expensive; while printers who sell their work cheaply must prefer simplicity.

Aldus Manutius, the greatest printer, could have delighted fastidious collectors, but chose to publish volumes that anyone could purchase. Through his innovation of the compact Italic type he was the first to print books of pocket size that could be held in one hand while being read. He sought to make knowledge universal, and felt that an author was imprisoned as long as he was confined to manuscript.[1] With the speed of the Dolphin and the tenacity of the Anchor, in his famous device, Aldus published 120 editions of revolutionary cheapness in twenty years.

His publications were chiefly classics, because in the fifteenth century there were few new books to

[1] Cf. Orcutt, William Dana, *Master Makers of the Book*, p. 72.

be printed, but mostly because he had the human-
istic enthusiasm for antiquity. The first printers
were scholars, and they required learned help in
their great effort to spread learning. Erasmus su-
pervised the issue of a number of classics for
Aldus, and later was proofreader for Froben. Erasmus was the greatest scholar of the Renaissance,
the most popular author of his day, and the first
man to support himself largely by writing. With
him the modern world broke into print. His *Praise
of Folly* was a better seller than any other book
except the Bible. Martin Luther vied with Erasmus
in popularity because the Reformation brought a
new reading public eager to read the reformers and
the Bible. Luther stimulated unprecedented reading of the Bible by exalting it in place of the
church as the final authority in religion, and by
urging every man to read the Scripture to decide
for himself what it meant. So the Word came to
be the printed word.

Now that the Bible can be obtained by anyone,
and printers have nearly realized Aldus' dream of
making knowledge universally available, the an-

swer to the question whether printing should be an expensive art or a cheap one is that it may be both. As in the case of the Bible, a luxurious edition of a book does not reduce the sharability of literature when there is also a popular edition of that book, as there is sure to be if there is a wide demand for it.

The Bible is still the best seller among what are called books, but it is not read nearly as much as the newspaper with its circulation in the millions. Any issue of a metropolitan daily, and of course the Sunday edition, is really a book in all but binding. If a book is "a number of sheets of paper bound or stitched together, especially a printed and bound volume,"[1] a magazine must be a book. Newspapers and magazines are the cheapest books, and constitute the reading matter of the largest public.

A man who goes through a newspaper in the morning and one in the evening has scant time for other reading. Even if he gets up early on Sunday he cannot finish the Sunday paper before the Mon-

[1] *Standard Dictionary*, Funk & Wagnalls.

day one comes. It is amusing to notice how many people, who use "bookish" as a term of reproach, bury themselves in newspapers whenever they have leisure. It is equally interesting to note how much time is spent on news sheets by people who think they have little value. Persons who feel that they are wasting their eyesight on print not in their precious tomes are repeatedly drawn by the latest headlines. A paper is easily picked up under the delusion that it can easily be laid down, when one would hesitate to open a book that would obviously occupy some time. Proust suggested binding newspapers handsomely and putting them on the shelf, and strewing important works in loose leaves on the table.

Newspapers are popular because they abound with values of lively human interest. Usually the first thing looked for in the paper is the meteorological report and forecast, because the mood of nature is very important to the human mind, and man wants to watch the vagaries of the weather even when protected from them. Many people are so shut in that "fair and warmer" or "snow and colder" is only what it looks like on paper, yet they are cheered or chilled to see it there. Events in foreign lands or in different wards of their own city are real for most people only if reported in the paper. Baseball fans who never sit in the bleachers follow the game from the sporting page. Many people feel richer or poorer after reading the financial page, and more than four hundred have *entrée* to exclusive circles through the Society Notes. Everyone wishes to know the things that would interest him, and perhaps nowhere else can so many of them be known as in the paper. The supreme facts of birth, marriage, and death are always there. One would wait in vain for a person to come along with half the news to be found in a single paper.

People like scientists, who have interests not adequately represented in the ordinary papers, find what is important news to them chiefly in professional journals and books. While scientists resort to experiment and do not rely unduly on reports, they are constantly inspired and guided by publications of other investigators and the records of

163

their predecessors. Without the aid of printing it is conceivable that science might fall back toward the old trial-and-error method of meeting difficulties, which alone is feasible when the individual is out of touch with the experience of his contemporaries and ancestors. Science is coöperative on a scale impossible without the printer's art. Not only is a worker in science unable to proceed far alone, but the results of his procedure are of no consequence until he has published them so that they can be examined and corroborated by other men.

In former days a man who discovered something was likely to be secretive and mysterious about it. The modern thinker knows that knowledge grows when pooled and shrinks when hoarded, and believes that the benefit of one is bound up with the good of all. He sees that the cause of enlightenment against all sorts of ignorance and unfairness has been tremendously advanced by the printing press. Though its liberty has been interfered with since its invention,[1] what is hushed up for a while gets printed sooner or later, if it is of general con-

[1] Cf. Oswald, John Clyde, *A History of Printing*, p. 71.

cern. "Hereby tongues are knowne, knowledge groweth, judgment encreaseth, books are dispersed, the Scripture is seene, the doctors be read, stories be opened, times compared, truth discerned, falshood detected, and with finger pointed, and all, as I said, through the benefit of Printing."[1]

Human evolution has reached the printing age. Our knowledge is chiefly a store of typographical signs enabling us to make adjustments to the environment and to solve our problems. William James said that the tigers in India are only marks on paper when we read about them, but if we pursued the meaning of these symbols we should eventually come to beasts actually prowling the jungle. We follow up the names of few animals, birds, flowers, trees, or stones beyond their appearance on the page unless our profession is that of zoölogist, ornithologist, botanist, or mineralogist, in which case we ourselves become something that is only a word to other people. The difference between war and peace, between making money

[1] From Fox's *Acts and Monuments*, quoted by Theodore L. De Vinne on the title page of *The Invention of Printing*.

and losing it, and between truth and falsehood, is a difference in the black and white of what we read. Seldom is it feasible or even possible to investigate further, because the printed version of the world is fairly reliable and because print constitutes our universe to such an extent that if we are uneasy about what we read in one place, often all that we can do is to read in other places. Many values that concern us have no local habitation where they could be hunted out like tigers, and like the God of the Bible are most nearly substantial in their printed names.

The reality of society itself resides today chiefly in print. Not only the constitutions and statutes which represent the permanent structure of society, but the changes and developments in its life, can be located most readily in print. Children are taught to read in order that they may be initiated into the group. One might say that the illiterate are honorary members of our society, like the dogs that ride in motor-cars and the cats that live in apartments. One can surely say that only people who read or are read to can really belong. Persons out of touch with print do not know the shibboleths which distinguish the modern man superficially, or the ideas that characterize him basically. Among primitive men the ceremonies by which the young are inducted into the tribe serve to pass on tradition and the wisdom of generations which are accumulated in the heads of the leaders. It is the same among civilized men today, except that much of what they wish their young to learn can be mastered only through acquaintance with books. Reading is no longer a pretty accomplishment, but is as necessary for us as for hunters to hunt or fishers to fish; and printing is as fundamental to our living as making arrows or nets could be to savage life.

Printing led to the discovery of a newer world than the one Columbus found, and it may be that Columbus used his caravels to transport printed volumes. Certainly the benefits of printing have been greatly aided by transportation. The telegraph, the wireless, and the postal system have all increased the importance of printing, as have cheap newspapers, free school books, and public libraries. But all these things could not have helped printing much, had it not progressed beyond the stamping on bricks of clay that formed the libraries of Babylonia and Assyria.

PART THREE

ART AND LIFE

Chapter Twelve

BUSINESS AND SCIENCE AS ART

IF BEAUTY is value contemplated, then it must appear not only in the realm of what are usually considered to be the fine arts, but wherever the imagination is caught by a vision of something better and beyond. Any intelligent and sensitive fitting together of means for the achievement of ends is art; any man who exercises skill and forethought in fulfilling a plan is an artist. The assumption that there are two kinds of activity divorced from each other, the practical and the æsthetic, has been unfortunate for all concerned, no matter which camp they have called theirs. In the effort to be purely practical, some men have despised fineness as frivolous and have become coarse; while in the attempt to be entirely æsthetic other men have disdained virility as vulgar and

171

have become soft. The world of work and affairs seems harsh, the world of art appears sentimental, because work, to be human, should be done with the lovingness of art; and art, to be manly, should be practiced with the seriousness of work. As a matter of fact, many men take the artist's attitude toward their business, and are sincerely interested in what is called art, not only as an escape from their daily occupation, but because they recognize and admire in it the characteristics of their own endeavor. At the same time artists feel that they are supplying fundamental needs as truly as the butcher and the baker.

The artificiality of the commonly accepted separation between practical and æsthetic pursuits is exposed when it is seen that the attributes of the one belong properly to the other. Æsthetic activity is that which is indulged in for its own sake, while practical activity is that which is engaged in for the sake of something ulterior. One pays at once, the other later. But it is equally practical to be chiefly interested in the bird in the hand; æsthetic to yearn for what is over the hill. It is practical to plan ahead and not to count chickens before they are hatched; it is æsthetic to contemplate things at a distance, remote from actuality, and also to sink sweetly into the sensation of the moment.

The reason that there has seemed to be a real difference between the two is that "practical" has come to apply to what must be done, "æsthetic" to what it might be nice to do if there were time, but which under the circumstances only irresponsible people would potter with. We have not been long removed from pioneer days when little energy was left over from providing food, clothing, and shelter. Throughout the history of the race, as well as during its long prehistorical evolution, existence has been precarious. Even when arrived far beyond the frontier stage the livelihood of most of mankind has been hard won and insecure. The life of recent man has been more strenuous than that of his less civilized or uncivilized ancestors. Unlike them, he has had to work without hunger or the excitement of the hunt, at work that has had no interest for him beyond the money that happened to come after it. He has not lingered over his handi-

173

work to embellish it; he has done only what his taskmasters have required, until the whistle blew, when he has been too tired for anything but rest or violent diversion. In leisure he has not dreamed of his labor, caressed and carved its tools. Yet little as he may have liked his employment, he has been haunted by the dread of losing it. His employers have not been much better off. Only apparently have they had more freedom, for they could not lay down the sword of responsibility.

Such absorption in "practical" affairs came about because the lot of man had been so difficult that no amount of industry could be regarded as excessive. So suddenly successful have our efforts been, however, that now we might be ensconced in security, if the fruits of science and industry were fairly distributed throughout society. If business were conducted as a social art and not as a selfish game, the many might share the comfort now monopolized by a few. Our control of nature is such that with social planning all men should have relief from the anxiety of making a living, and have leisure to enjoy life, like children and artists.

An awakening to the delight that the world is crammed with might still be troubled by the influence of Calvinistic religion, which relegated enjoyment to a remote future, demanding that the present be emptied of pleasure and filled with work. This religion further became the ally of the practical life by deeming worldly success to be the mark of divine favor. Now the possibilities of the present are breeding impatience with the doctrine that good things are to be had only in another world. Science is discrediting the superstitions of religion, and for science to teach that life cannot be enjoyed is now more serious than for religion to say it must not.

Many thoughtful people believe that such is the teaching of science. They think that science gives a truer though harsher picture of reality than religion, that it puts away fancies and gets down to facts that can be impartially observed, recorded, and corroborated. They see science experimenting and testing to get away from what is individual and local to the universal and abstract. They see objects and human beings themselves dematerializing into electrical wraiths. They stretch their minds to comprehend the astronomical and atomical universes, and in neither do they find any comfort for man. The sciences that deal with man himself, as an individual and as a member of society, are almost as chilling, since they also put their findings as far as possible into abstruse, quantitative terms.

When life is a routine of impersonal relations, and the high priests of knowledge report that the world is even colder and more heartless than it seems, it is no wonder that people crave the illusion of color, though at bottom it be nothing but colorless wave-lengths; that they seek love, though it be nothing but the stimulation of reflexes. If man is a machine, he must still have rest, and he must have calories and vitamins if not food. The proof that he is not a machine, or that if he is one he is a human machine, is that he needs comfort and affection, encouragement and hope. He must feel some warm response from his environment.

176

If he cannot find it in reality he must invent it in daydream.

The daydreams called religion have been discredited by science, because they have claimed to have reality; but those of art have been spared because they have professed to be make-believe. Science would not brook a rival truth, but it could not quarrel with fantasy. If children and women and artists wished to waste their time on idle toys, there was no great harm in it so long as the efficiency of laboratories and factories was not impaired. The tired scientist, as well as the tired business man, might even refresh himself with art after hours. For a sane man, who might have been a practical person, to go in seriously for art was a scandal.

It is significant then that John Dewey, the philosopher of science and practice, who has never had anything to do with religion, has capitulated to beauty and espoused the cause of art, saying that a work of art "is as much a case of genuine thought as that expressed in scientific and philosophical matters, and so is all genuine æsthetic appreciation of art, since the latter must in some way, to be vital, retrace the course of the creative process";[1] and that "scientific thought is in its turn a specialized form of art."[2] Einstein regards his science as art. Similarly, many men of affairs will admit that their business is a game if not an art, and when they spend their money it is often on art. Finally, the popular interest in art has grown to the point where an artist is more often admired than ridiculed.

Art has established itself so strongly that it does not need to justify itself to science. The scientists are saying so themselves, confessing that they cannot live in a purely scientific world of formulas and pointer readings. We are beginning to wonder why anyone should have tried to live in such a world. Mr. Dewey has shown the reason to be that science was supposed to be giving a picture of reality, and that whatever science might reveal reality to be, we should have to live in it. Now it appears that science has not been picturing reality

[1] "Qualitative Thought," in *The Symposium*, January, 1930, p. 32.
[2] *Ibid.*, p. 17.

178

so much as abstracting those aspects of the world that would enable us to control it with reference to our purposes.

The scientist does not mean that calories and vitamins, which have no taste, are more real than the food we eat. But by thinking in such terms he has varied and enriched our fare. The scientific statement of food is not a substitute for things to eat or a rival to them; it is a means to making eatables more abundant and satisfying. Blueprints of houses are not more real than the dwellings we inhabit; they are a means toward building houses. A map of the world is a tool to facilitate going from place to place, and it is more helpful for being bare of houses, trees, and weather, but does not deny their existence. An anatomical drawing of a man serves purposes that a portrait would not, but is not truer. It has truth, it refers to traits of reality, but it is absurd to suppose that it represents the whole truth of reality. Art rather than science strives to give a picture of the world, that it may be contemplated as a whole, with all its interest

179

and color. Science is more concerned to solve problems. Its pictures are mechanical drawings, architect's plans, outlines. Works of art have more soul and body, because designed to represent human experience vividly. Science abstracts from qualities and deals chiefly with quantities—but for the purpose of enhancing qualities. So instead of being antagonistic to values, science secures and increases them, which is to say that science is not very different from art.

Science was born of such arts as divination, healing, farming, and building, and continues to be the development of techniques whereby they may flourish. "Pure" science is as mythical as mere machinery. A laboratory is not a jumble of test-tubes and retorts any more than a factory is a confusion of belts and wheels. In each is an order governed by the problems of practical life that are being solved there. But science is an art in the sense of being developed for its own sake, as well as in being instrumental to the achievement of social ends. The scientist is now so aware of the practical

justification of his work that he feels safe in vaunt-
ing its intrinsic interest. This may even be the heart
of his devotion to science, causing him to resent
emphasis upon its utility and to distinguish invidi-
ously between the "pure" scientist and the mere
technician, though he must know that the purest
science has its use. A geologist, in advising a business man, may feel pride in helping him to solve
a problem for the intellectual satisfaction of knowing how, but may feel that if the man goes ahead
and makes a million dollars, it is his fault.

Some scientists blush for the utility of science
because (though in its difficult beginnings it was
of so little use that its "æsthetic" aspect had to be
played up) now that its usefulness is obvious,
many of its devotees are artistic persons who go
into it chiefly for love of the harmonies to be designed and discovered there, expecting, since they
work in laboratories instead of in studios, to escape
being accused of "ivory tower" æstheticism. Many
scientists feel free to say that they do not care
whether their achievements can be applied in prac-

tice, because the common man believes, in spite of their statements, that they are helping the world along. As long as they lay golden eggs most people will not suspect that they are artists.

Rarely is this suspected of business men, but their work would not be practical were it not æsthetic in the sense of aiming toward intrinsic value; and activity leading to value can hardly fail to be valued in itself. Business is practical because it makes money, and money is practical because with it can be had things desirable for their own sake, such as the comfort and education of one's family, security, and prestige. Men are calculating and close-fisted in their affairs in order to be generous and open-handed at home and with their friends. It is only when reduced to their lowest terms that means and ends are divorced. Work which is nothing more than the means of making a living, from which little more than a living can be derived, is naturally shirked or deserted when possible; but more absorbing work may become the main interest in life. Such is the work of scientists, artists, ministers, and successful business men. After it has made money or brought about other ends for which work is done, it is not abandoned, but is continued for its own sake. A man may plan for the perpetuation of his business not only beyond his lifetime, but when he sees that it must pass out of the hands of his family and friends; just as a scientist, a prophet, or an artist expects his achievements to survive him and to be supplemented by others.

Since work is significant as a means to things that have meaning, the more important its results the more worth while it becomes, until it may become more meaningful than any of the things it leads to. The more important the consequences of an enterprise, the greater will be the love and thought devoted to it and the more it will have need of them, until it becomes so refined and complicated that it requires affection to be understood and rewards understanding with enriched emotion. Then the means have justly become the end.

To live for such work is not to narrow life, but

to broaden it, and to overcome the schism between the practical and the æsthetic. Activity is impractical in so far as it falls short of the directly satisfying; hence unæsthetic in so far as it fails to be practical. An artist who paints just to make a living, and does not succeed, or succeeds only in sustaining a life that has no interest but the effort to sustain itself, is not only a failure as a practical person but as an artist. A business man who makes far more than a living, and whose life is concentrated on developing and extending its operations for their own sake, is not only being conspicuously practical, but thoroughly artistic. A poor artist is only a bad business man; a bad business man is a poor artist.

Science is allied to business, enabling it to strengthen its control over nature for the welfare of man; and, like business, science has much in common with art—as skill in solving practical problems and in bringing order out of chaos. Science holds those theories to be truest that achieve the neatest coiffure of disheveled facts. Some wisp of fact eludes the deftest fingers, and men of science know that soon their mistress will appear with her hair all down again; but they are not disturbed, knowing that such is the way of nature, that tresses which stay in place are artificial, and seem real because they are false.

Science and business may share with art the religious attribute of consecration to a cause, involving discipline, humility, and heroism. There may be in the laboratory and the office the asceticism and concentration of the monastic cell; the same loyalty to great names, and passion to do better than the fathers. Apostles of industry, missionaries teaching agriculture and medicine, may be as sincere and enlightened as any harbingers of civilization. At the same time religion is trying to be scientific and business-like. It cannot carry on without discarding creeds and facing the problems of educated as well as ignorant people. Nor can it operate without an efficient organization and adequate budget, for which it relies largely on men of business.

Of course it is only because different activities have distinctive traits that it is worth while to uncover their common character; but different as they are upon the surface, they are identical at bottom. The æsthetic and the practical are phases of that originally undifferentiated experience which is ever human, and always capable of beauty.

Chapter Thirteen

PHILOSOPHY AND RELIGION AS ART

THE artistic nature of all intelligent living and
the consequent ubiquity of beauty, are implicit in
the discovery that business and science are not beyond the pale of art, but are explicit in philosophy
and religion. If art is the solving of problems and
the representation of values to be contemplated,
then philosophy and religion are art, and there
can be no art above them, unless it be that of life
itself. But life breathes through the arts, which
begin with religion and culminate in philosophy.
Everything in life is drawn up into philosophy and
religion. To try to escape them is only to go more
deeply into them. They are life at its livest. They
are the quick of existence.

Like all art, philosophy and religion strive to
overcome ugliness, though often they seem to ca-

187

pitulate to it. A common cause of wonder is that many rare souls are deeply troubled, that those able to get the most from life should find much of it unattractive. It is more wonderful that their suffering may be the very thing that shows us their fineness, for we associate wisdom and sensitiveness with disillusion and melancholy. We think of philosophers and saints as aloof from the vanity of the world. We say that ignorance is bliss and despise bliss. We would rather be Socrates dissatisfied than a fool satisfied, though we know that philosophy and virtue are not the only sources of discontent.

Democritus alone is known as the laughing philosopher, and what amused him was the disproportion between man's self-importance and his place in the universe. Plato turned away from Athens to live in a world of ideas, because that city had put to death the best and wisest of men. Aristotle held that a worth-while life could belong to only a few, and refused to judge any man happy until after his death. The Cyrenaics reduced living to the satisfaction of the most elemental desires, regarding social obligation as a foolish addition to

188

the burden of life. The Cynics scoffed at refinement, were proud of their rags, and slept in the street. The Epicureans found pleasure chiefly in the absence of pain, and were no blither than the Stoics, who have always typified the philosophic way of life. The Skeptics taught that neither the senses nor reason could be trusted for the truth. Plotinus and the mystical philosophers, pagan and Christian, maligned everything pertaining to the body or the world, except as symbols of another realm of being, of which all that they could say was that nothing could be said. The mediæval thinkers generally taught that this life could be good only as preparation for another.

Since Descartes philosophers have built up a world view based on science, so coldly intellectual that they have sought escape from it in a non-scientific sphere of values, which either has no connection with science, hence no reality for them, or emanates therefrom and so is cheerless like science. Some modern philosophers have tried to avoid this trouble by regarding the "real" world of science as a shadow of the ideal world, only to land in skepticism. Kant attempted to escape this predicament by affirming the necessity of behaving *as if* there were both a world of science and of values, while he showed the impossibility of proving the existence of either. Following Kant's conception that the world of things in themselves is unknowable and that the world of appearance is constituted by human thought, came Fichte, Schelling, and Hegel, who all regarded reality as the creation of the self. Schopenhauer found in this creative activity the source of woe, complaining that there was no point to creating for the sake of creating, that nothing could appease the will, since whatever it attained, it craved something further.

Pragmatism has also taught that the main thing in life is to get ahead. Like many ancient systems, it is so pessimistic about the possibility of knowing the ultimate nature of things, that it dismisses conventional metaphysics as a waste of time. It is sanguine about the importance of science, and devotes much attention to progress in social welfare, which accounts for the pragmatic test of truth—that a theory is true if and in so far as it works. By that test we cannot always know what to eat or wear, let alone what to think, because we can accustom ourselves to very strange things, and, having done so, it is hard to change our habits. We may suspect that habits which work smoothly may prevent us from trying other methods that later might work better, since at first the new would never seem as good as the old. When the better appears first in guise of the worse, how shall we recognize it? But experiment is justified of her children, and Pragmatism says that we must have faith in change. We must will to believe in progress, though sometimes this "will to believe" is no less desperate than Kant's heroic "as if."

Does Pragmatism work? Within the realm of everyday experience it has served well enough, and outside that realm it has nothing to say. But Pragmatists themselves cannot help being curious about the background of life, feeling that if they knew more about it, their activities in the foreground might have different significance. What is the use of progress? What is progress? Such questions, vital to practical life, cannot be answered without looking beyond it. H. G. Wells says in *Meanwhile* that life would not be worth living were it not for the hope that it might be ameliorated in the future.

The upshot of the optimistic philosophy of Pragmatism might seem to be pessimism. According to this doctrine thought is for action, and action is for the sake of further action. Pragmatists see that the value of thought and of action is to make life more worth living; they admit that social welfare is meaningless if it does not mean individual welfare; but of this what can be known without a long look before and after? Is the good always to be postponed to another generation? That is pessimism. What good is there which can be made sure of now, that will not disappoint us later?

John Dewey, in his *Human Nature and Conduct*, points out the folly of despising the present to live only for the future, which, when it arrives, turns out to be another despised present. He says that present meaning is what makes life worth while, that the value of future good lies in its significance here and now. For him the present is not a knife-edge, but ample enough to include recollection, anticipation, and a wide observation of what is in process of going on. In so far as the present is deprived of the value of activity, antecedent, immediate, and to be, life is emptied of interest. Present insight is what counts for Dewey: "There is no limit to the amount of meaning which reflective and meditative habit is capable of importing into even simple acts, just as the most splendid successes of the skillful executive who manipulates events may be accompanied by an incredibly meager consciousness."[1] Doing things for others will do them no good unless it widens their horizon and intensifies their perception. Doing things for oneself is equally futile unless it feeds the imagination and understanding. The results which Dewey values lie in the enrichment of present awareness. All else is vanity.

The dean of Pragmatists disapproves ideals and goals that must remain distant. He believes that constantly postponing meaning into the future is to sink it in a pit. For him the hope of happiness lies in present appreciation of what has been, what

[1] *Human Nature and Conduct,* p. 209.

is, and what is to be. The mere presence of an object is of no importance without awareness of its significance; and the absence of a thing is no loss when the essence of it is secured by the mind. But through reflection the Pragmatist finds significance in unreflective activity that may be enjoyed directly, without thinking. For him the purpose of thought is to enhance life on all its levels. John Dewey says: "The chief function of philosophy is to free men's minds from bias and prejudice and to enlarge their perception of the world about them."[1]

The Pragmatist is like other philosophers, however, in that what most interests him is perceiving the process of thought, thinking about thinking. The joy of understanding is the treasure that will not rust or wither. According to the most pessimistic thinkers, wisdom is worth living for, and alone makes life worth while. In the realm of ideas, which is only the ordinary world as thought about, all values may be enjoyed up to the limit of human appreciation, and perhaps there is none.

[1] *The Philosophy of John Dewey*, edited by Joseph Ratner, p. 525.

Action is an idea in so far as it has a meaning that we can contemplate, and Schopenhauer himself found solace in the world as idea. There everything is attained, and even the restless will is an idea. That ideas may be the product of the will, does not detract from their ideality, but adds one more idea to be contemplated.

Wise and saintly men are often called pessimistic because they discount what are commonly deemed the pleasures of life, but they build up an ideal world in which we also may love to dwell. That world consists not so much in a region apart as in a fresh perspective upon mundane things whereby they suddenly outshine all that we had thought bright before. This insight of men whose vision appears distorted to the unseeing, is like the art of El Greco—the darker it paints, the fairer the beauty it reveals.

For wise men common life is holy ground, the soil from which beauty springs. When the vulgar and the ugly are recognized as the matrix of the beautiful, they are no longer sordid. But it was necessary that they should have seemed so, else beauty might not have transpired; for beauty is value contemplated, and value always appears in contrast to things of little worth. If there were no death, life would not be precious; and if death were nothing real, to swallow it up would not be a victory.

Unamuno has shown how bitter life may be without philosophy and religion to draw hope from despair and find comfort in tears. He feels that Shakespeare's saying that we are such stuff as dreams are made on, is more tragic than Calderón's saying that life is a dream; because Shakespeare makes *us* nothing but dreams that dream.[1] We might object that even as the Greeks cared not what elements their gods were said to be made of, so long as they had their gods, it should not matter to us what we ourselves be made of, so long as we continue to be ourselves. But what disturbs Unamuno is the fear that we may not continue. He wants "*to be*, to be forever, to be without end; he has a thirst for being, a thirst for being more, a hunger for God, a thirst for eternalizing and eter-

[1] Unamuno, Miguel de, *Del Sentimiento Trágico de la Vida*, p. 42.

nal love, to be forever, to be God! . . . This thought that I have to die and the enigma of what must take place afterward is the very palpitation of my consciousness. Contemplating a serene green field, or looking into clear eyes in which appears a soul that is sister to mine, my consciousness dilates, feeling the diastole of the soul, and I breathe deep the life around me, and I believe in my future; but instantly the voice of the mystery whispers to me, You will cease to be! I am grazed by the wing of the Angel of death, and the systole of the soul inundates my spiritual bowels with the blood of divinity."[1]

Unamuno is mad—as Don Quixote was mad, as the mystics were mad—with a divine madness, and what he says passionately is what philosophers say calmly. He quotes from the sixth proposition in the third part of the *Ethics* of Spinoza, *"Unaquaeque res, quatenus in se est, in suo esse perseverare conatur"*; which is to say that everything in so far as it exists in itself, strives to persist in its existence. Yet was Spinoza calm? the God-in-

[1] *Ibid.*, p. 43.

toxicated man! The tranquillity of the philosophic mind is only apparent. Though it seeks the truth, it hopes to find that truth is the same as beauty, that what the head can accept is what the heart yearns for, as if there were no contradiction. That way madness lies, and Unamuno does not hesitate to say that consciousness is a disease peculiar to man, the sick ape. He says that intelligence is man's compensation for weakness, that the more ills he can suffer and tolerate, the more subtle his intelligence becomes in the effort to restore him to the brute's dreamy harmony with his world, the untroubled faith of the animal. But when the crafty int elect is not subtle enough, it aggravates man's discomfort instead of relieving it, and exaggerates the terror of death, which does not bother the beast. For man to save himself through thinking (and he has no other way) is almost impossible, because thought not only must direct the body (in animals self-sufficient) but guide itself. Thinking discovers so many difficulties that the heart fain would dismiss the head, for it cannot rest while the head, wearing the crown of consciousness, lies uneasy. This gives all men and all peoples the tragic sense of life.

Yet were there no doubt, there could be no faith; as there could be no values without problems. The faith of common people is as natural as the animal's at-homeness in the world. They are more simple and trusting than fancy folk; it is easier for them to pray, to believe, and to forget. They are not fretted by the discomforts of consciousness. But people endowed with vivid consciousness are compensated in being closer to the faith of the philosopher, untroubled by vicissitudes that would shatter the trust of the ignorant, who are always in danger of becoming aware of some frightful doubt that could be dispelled only by trained thought. A philosopher is able to see good where others could not find it, or to reconcile himself to inevitable evil. He is snugger in his philosophy than an animal in his fur.

Philosophy is not a private approach to truth, a secret access to reality. It tries to correlate what the sciences discover, and to see life whole. Each science selects a corner of the world for study and becomes so specialized that when men of different sciences gather about the table in a faculty club they cannot understand one another unless they talk about their newspapers and the weather, their wives and children. Yet they are curious about one another's work, and each feels isolated if he cannot to some extent tell his colleagues what most interests him. To explain, he must put his ideas on the table, make diagrams on the cloth, use knives and forks as symbols, and try to speak in terms as plain as bread and butter. So it becomes evident to the philosopher that all special knowledge, which has branched off from common experience, must return thither to recover human significance.[1] Even in his own laboratory the scientist proceeds by interpreting the unknown in terms of what is known to him, and his interpretation seems strange only because most people are unacquainted with what to him is familiar. Sometimes the layman is surprised by the simplicity of scientific thought: the physiologist wonders whether a nerve functions as a pipe, a rope, a fuse, or an electric wire; the

[1] Cf. Ames, Edward Scribner, *Religion*, p. 67.

physicist whether light is transmitted in streams or in waves. The scientist is like the poet in trying to find expressive figures; and he cannot be satisfied until he can communicate his findings to his fellows and contribute to a view of life that all can share.

Philosophy, however, is more than a synthesis of the sciences. Whatever concerns mankind is its province. It does not try to know all the facts, but teaches the futility of information without wisdom. Philosophy takes men up into the high places, showing them that since they can identify themselves with anything that interests them, they may be saved by devoting themselves to things that endure—community, country, and race. These and the earth itself may disappear, but only to be absorbed in the universe, which must be everlasting, since it is always that which is, whatever form it takes or leaves. In a sense even the forms, which from a finite point of view are assumed and abandoned, are eternal, because nothing can alter the fact that all possible shapes are always the same, whether or not they are swimming in the ocean of occurrence.

Thus to contemplate things under the aspect of eternity is the function of philosophy. To consider in one sweep all that appears or disappears or never appears is its majestic response to the problem of life.

Philosophy at its best is a way of living as well as a kind of learning, enabling man to be at home in the universe and at ease in eternity. Like a dog in the sun or a cat by the fire, the philosopher spreads peacefulness to others, not so much by act or word as by serenity and silence. He need not do anything overt that can be valued, or say anything aloud that can be followed; unmoved, his calmness moves; unuttered, his thoughts speak out.

Philosophy is thus not very different from religion. The one emphasizes more the head, the other more the heart, but in a balanced life the two are fused. Philosophers have manifested religious zeal in their teaching; and in their preaching, religious leaders have shown philosophical insight. The philosopher or minister who can save souls does not deceive; he teaches nothing that he cannot be sure of, and does not pretend to know what he cannot believe. Jesus told his disciples to be as cunning as serpents and as gentle as doves, that they might know the worst, yet believe the best.

Wise men know the genesis of values without ceasing to value them. Supposing that man did come up from the slime, he is man for a' that, if not because of that. If his heaven is an idea, it is none the less ideal. Jesus said, "The Kingdom of God is within you." He said that it would not come in an obvious way, because it was not to be a physical state, but a spiritual one. He was not optimistic enough to think that everyone could attain it, for he said, "Strait is the way and narrow is the gate, and few there be that find it." He believed that the poor in spirit would always be with us, and theirs was the only poverty that distressed him. At the same time he believed that whoever drank of his words would never thirst, that no one who would purify himself and believe in him would ever die.

What he meant was what great prophets and philosophers have always meant, and like them he has been greatly misunderstood. People have interpreted his sayings literally, despite his disparagement of literalness. They have imagined a material heaven and a temporal immortality, as if there were anything spiritual in that. Science has done religion a good turn in making such notions ridiculous as well as immoral, though most people think that they have lost their religion when they are no longer able to believe what no enlightened person could believe. Only the sophisticated can distinguish between the spirit and the letter of religion. When they see that beauty, even heavenly beauty, consists in the contemplation of value, they are not disturbed to know that beauty is not made of gold or jewels or anything substantial. They accept the idea that beauty does not exist except in idea. When they discover the nature of beauty they do not cease to love it. When they know that eternity is timeless they see the possibility of becoming eternal, and no longer confuse it with a bodily survival of endless duration. Could a man be saved by living forever? Were he saved, could he be lost by dying? A man need not wait until death to enter heaven. He may enter now, at any moment, whenever he sees beauty.

Everyone enters heaven who beholds beauty. When Michelangelo said that Ghiberti's bronze doors were worthy to be the gates of Paradise, he meant what he said, for Paradise, with all its mansions, is a creation of art. Many people will think that a work of art could not be divine, ignoring that the very notion of divinity is an artistic construction. They are like the Jews who forbade graven images, because they were idols, when their whole worship was directed toward verbal images. Are the images of poets any less idols than those of sculptors? Poetry may be more divine than sculpture only if it be finer, more compassionate and searching. Religion and philosophy cannot be discredited for being poetry, but for sometimes being poor poetry. Only as art can religion and philosophy have any value, any beauty, any truth. Is there any truth that is not a work of art? If there be, only as it becomes art can we be persuaded of its truth.

The good, the right, the divine, to which religion would inspire devotion, are admired in art as the beautiful. The difference would be merely verbal, were it not that often words with an odor of sanctity are sniffed with suspicion by seemingly emancipated people whom words redolent of paganism do not offend. A person may even go to church without compromising his intellectual standing with anti-religious people if he says that his interest is not religious, but æsthetic. If he goes for the architecture, the music, the poetry, the pageantry of it, he is beyond reproach. The lover of beauty goes to the fine arts for the same reason that people used to go to church, to be soothed and exalted. Instead of denying his heart, he discovers in art the comfort and excitement that his like used to find in religion.

If the attraction of art is hardly distinguishable from that of religion, it is legitimate for churches to avail themselves of the appeal of the arts. Having admitted the value of art, one must concede the importance of religion as art. To differentiate between religion and the arts on the ground that the arts are godless is futile (aside from the fact of godless religions), because the presence of God in religion means, so far as a meaning can be found, that in religion people are quieted and excited far above the ordinary. In art they are affected the same way, but do not attribute it to the presence of God.

There is little difference between attending a church service and going to a concert, except that one experience is termed religious, the other æsthetic. In both there is a change from the usual world, and the sense that upon return to it there must ever after be something unusual about it. In both there is a shift from taking things merely as signs of other things, or just for granted, to absorbing the full significance of everything and realizing that everything is significant. In church or at a concert there is relief, the goal is reached, eternity is now. Here we are released from doing to being. All we have ever done or can ever do, all that is forever beyond our range, is near us now.

Art is persuasion. Art can carry away the cynical, assure them of harmony between head and heart, convince them of the value of life and of its triumph over death, win them to the spiritual essence of religion, and show them that only the spirit matters, that the spirit cannot be false or unreal, because it is ideal. Such was the art of Jesus. It was so compelling that the skeptical Romans were won to him.

The divinity of Christ was his irresistible humanity, his intelligent sympathy, his power to comfort and give rest. He led people to heal themselves by faith and forgetfulness. He taught that when the dread of death is overcome, death is vanquished. The Epicureans and Stoics had taught this, but in such chilling fashion that life itself seemed a lingering death. The Man of Sorrows cast out fear and melancholy, laughed at care, and told people not to worry about the morrow, but to be like the birds of the air and the lilies of the field. He enjoyed living and spread the joy of it. He liked to feast with friends, and to fast in solitude. He found beauty in the street and in the garden. He loved to talk with men and to walk with God. Wherever he went he felt that he was in the Father and that the Father was in him.

He saw that nothing matters, because in the sight of God the last is like the first and the strong is like the weak; and he saw that nothing is in vain, because the hairs on our heads are numbered, and not a sparrow falls to the ground without God's knowledge. No one can doubt this in the presence of beauty, and who has really beheld beauty will see it everywhere.

Chapter Fourteen

THE ART OF LOVE

LOVERS feel that people who seek salvation in philosophy and religion are those who have missed love, or lost it. The extent to which philosophers and saints use the language of love to describe their experience is a recognition of its significance. Their insistence that their way of life is better than that of love is indicative that ordinarily the way of love is best. At least they will admit that human love is an adumbration of the divine. How can he love God whom he has not seen who does not love man whom he has seen?

To come together without any reservation is to be lovers. We are indifferent or polite, if not hostile, to most people; but toward those with whom we have something in common we unbend. Friendship grows out of shared experience. Except for common interests friends may be strangers, unsympathetic and reticent. As Santayana says, people are friends in spots. But they are lovers all over. Only lovers can be together without hiding anything, secure in the joy of being accepted for what they really are; free of the usual fear of giving themselves away or being found out.

The intimacy of two people is as great as the inhibitions surmounted by them. Since the most serious inhibitions usually are between the sexes, the deepest love will normally be heterosexual, though the assumption that this is normal is what makes homosexual relations interesting. Nothing equals the discovery that man and woman can be together as if there were no difference of man and woman between them, unless it be the discovery that two of the same sex can be to each other as if their sexes were different. When Virginia Woolf's Orlando has turned into a woman she says to her lover, unbelieving that a man could be as sympathetic as he, "Are you a woman?" and he says to her, "Are you a man?"

Society holds the sexes so much apart that it

seems natural to suppose an opposition between them almost amounting to warfare. When a young man first goes courting, he is anxious lest the slightest disarrangement of his clothing or fault in his manner betray him to the enemy. A young lady, at the beginning of her conquests, is no less apprehensive of any irregularity in dress or behavior that might possibly be humiliating. Since, according to the code, she must be the pursued, she zealously avoids the appearance of pursuing by making her suitor (and as many males as she can) wait for her and upon her to the limit of patience. This strengthens his suspicion that he is not dealing with a friend, and may determine him to break down her defense, in sport or in earnest. To fall in love with the opponent under such conditions is indeed a fall, and may well be ridiculed as loss of independence and dignity.

After more or less accepting this conventional picture of the relation between the sexes, it comes like a revelation that a man and woman may cease to be foes and become more than friends; that instead of arming against each other they may bare their hearts in confidence. Then things that each had feared might be disillusioning may be endearing. Should she notice a spot on his suit, instead of being chagrined, he would be glad that she and not some one else had seen it, because now she is on his side. For creatures who had been foreign to each other to find peace in each other's presence is as wonderful as for a denizen of the jungle and a son of civilization to put faith in one another— as remarkable as for an elephant to relax his trunk at the approach of the man he trusts.

The fear that romance will end when marriage shall begin comes from imagining that the romantic is opposed to the real things of everyday. Most people start out with a moonlight conception of love, as if lovers should be like those in story books and movies. They try to be such themselves, but know the impossibility of keeping up the sham, and fear that before long they will come down to earth. If they continue to prize make-believe above the truth, they must be disillusioned, wistfully recalling the time of courtship and engagement, or solacing themselves with romances. But if they are

213

healthy and wholesome, lovers may discover the romance of reality, doffing their adolescent "ideals" as they would masquerade costumes. Reveling in facts, people cannot regret their fancies, and certainly not their fears.

The frequent fear that charm may vanish when mystery gives way to familiarity is justified if the breathlessness of occasional encounters is valued above the pleasure of daily companionship. But those who love to be together would prefer not to be always beginning over. First contacts cannot forever be exciting, not only because they must become an old story, but because their excitement being chiefly a premonition of continued intimacy, if that does not follow, they degenerate into false alarms. On the other hand, those who live intimately together find that habituation to each other submerges for periods the passionate lovers in them, so that when intermittently they awake to each other as such, their situation is analogous to that of reunion after absence.

There are unsuspected problems, but none that cannot be met with humor, intelligence, and tact, once the surprising truth dawns that lovers can be friends. All is well when it transpires that what, in the mist of ignorance, had seemed an unnatural situation is the most natural in the world. To leave father and mother, brother and sister, saying, "Where thou goest, I will go," is not appalling when in one person is found the essence of relative and friend, when, wherever he goes, one is not away from home. It also happens, and by no miracle, that former dear ones remain precious, that everything one had valued before continues to be treasured. Then to look back upon a step that had appeared as final as going over Niagara Falls in a barrel, to realize that one is still safe inside oneself and no whit different, to see that life is still ahead—is to laugh with the gods.

Mating is so natural that it may be wondered why there should be an art of love. As well ask why the naturalness of eating does not dispense with cooking; why the instinctiveness of play does not shut out sport; why the nativeness of speech does not rule out rhetoric; why the innateness of any capacity does not obviate the cultivation of it.

The reason that the animals take things as they come, at their lowest terms, without bothering about art, is that they are easily contented. Awareness of something ever beyond, awareness of value, is human. To believe in value is always to yearn for something better than what has been achieved. Contemplated, value is beauty. Attained, it escapes into new beauty, and the means of attaining beauty is art. Because art accompanies the effort to approach beauty, there is an art of love. Indeed, every art is an art of love, since every beauty is beloved.

Inasmuch as the beauty of the beloved increases with the devotion of the lover, the devotion can never be adequate to the beauty. The more he loves a woman the more a man feels that he cannot love her enough. Beginning with needing her selfishly and being good to her in order that she may cherish him, he becomes more genuinely interested in her until he really tries to put consideration for her first. For her to love him unselfishly makes him ever less egoistic in his attentiveness, which arouses deepening love in her. Soon nothing he does for her can appease the growing desire to delight her, and to please her increasingly alone can please him. The more each gives, the more the other gives. Very quickly in the reality of such a relationship a man and woman outsoar the romantic dreams of boy and girl. In retrospect the rosiest of those visions are poor and vaporous compared with the substantiality of mature experience. Sweet as they may be, they have a park-bench awkwardness and shyness that cannot be as sweet as the freedom, the inventiveness, and abandon of full-blown love.

Regarding love, more has been left unsaid than undone, but there is less foolishness in what has been done than in what has been said. Information anent affairs amorous must be inconsequential, because it concerns the most personal of matters. Delicacies of sentiment that can scarcely be remembered, that certainly cannot be reduced to rule, are the food of love. The most trivial things that lovers experience may become loaded with emotion, and half their value consist in the consciousness of their nothingness to others. While lovers are influenced by notions of what lovers should be, they like to behave in unsuspected ways. They forget

217

that they are lovers or husband and wife when not reminded by outsiders, since together they are simply themselves, and advice is not needed for that.

But while the uniqueness of their relation makes it hard for a third person to advise them, the happiness of lovers depends upon their own thoughtfulness. Unpremeditated tenderness is not more touching than consideration. Yet it is difficult to distinguish, because what was deliberate may become spontaneous, and what was discovered by accident may be repeated on purpose—if lovers do not forget before they can repeat, on account of the mysterious rapidity with which vivid experience fades. Unable to recall the ecstasy of a moment ago, the unreality of it makes them wonder whether it occurred. Distressing though this be, herein lies the possibility of ever renewed sweetness. Because one cannot remember every fleeting expression on the face of the beloved, it is a joy to search that face again and again for this and that forgotten look.

The sensation of actually loving is so evanescent that to be in love is mostly to have faith that one

218

will love, the next time one is with the beloved; as to like strawberries is to believe that they will taste good the next time one eats them, and certainly is not to taste them continually. To be fond of sport or reading or what not is to be sure that upon occasion the forgotten feel of it will come back with zest, as to be alive consists mainly in the confidence that one is going to live some more. In love and in life there is a rhythm of waking and sleeping, and who shall say which is the sweeter?

Much of what the head forgets is otherwise remembered—the tenderness of letters and of whispers in the night, summer fragrance, purity of snow—all that lovers share is theirs forever. The lovely moments that would not stay are heaped and poured into the present. In the life of lovers every experience is set off against the background of their past, or merged into it; everything that comes to them is compared or contrasted with that which went before. What had been only a note here and there, or a furtive melody, becomes a motive in a symphony in which are orchestrated the reverberations of their years together.

Often a young lover is troubled by fear of fickleness, knowing that had he not happened to know his love, he would be loving another. He must say to himself that since he is completely in love with her he could not have been more in love with anyone else, so that the only advantage which another girl could have would be the charm of novelty. Since this charm could not last, there would be nothing gained in changing to her. Were he now to see his own love as a stranger she would arouse his curiosity as much as any unknown; and if he should succeed in knowing her he would love her as he does now. After living happily with her for a time, their experience in common will make it impossible for another woman to take her place.

Besides becoming indispensable and induplicable she may also become fascinatingly unfamiliar. Mysteries about her, undiscernible in the novitiate of love, come more to the surface, only to suggest further subtleties beyond. The more he knows her the more he loves her, and the more he loves, the more there is to know, so that through the years the pursuit of her personality inspires and challenges all the imagination that he has. Who loves lightly can readily reach his aim, but he who loves deeply will learn that in a few months or years cannot be attained the last refinement of affection; and this is the first lesson in the art of love.

Some people feel that amorousness is all right for a season, but not for a lifetime. Shaw in *Back to Methuselah* says that if man lived long enough to grow up he would put away a childish thing like love and turn to higher mathematics. Wells in *Men Like Gods* suggests that the love theme has been dominant in literature on account of the preeminence in the world of people in their twenties. Now that an increasing number of mankind outlive adolescence and often outdo the young in benefit to society, life's center of gravity has shifted twenty years. To feel with Cabell that existence is not worth while after nineteen, except for recalling the palpitations of puppy love, seems a bit adolescent; and nothing shows more plainly the maturing of the race than the condescension now contained in that adjective referring to the period formerly regarded as the prime of life. To people with an inkling of the rich experience to be shared by lovers in the modern world, the sensuous love of Romeo and Juliet was a threadbare passion on which it was a shame for Shakespeare to waste his poetry. They hardly knew each other, much less anything else. More significant now is the love of Abélard and Héloïse, who were as far from being "Platonic," but who had the intellectual companionship reflected in their famous letters. Such a love could not be overestimated.

To love a person should be to love the friends, the activities and interests that constitute another self; but those who have no interest except in each other are shut in a house without windows, where there is no escape from ennui. Because Paolo cared only for Francesca and she only for him, they had nothing in common to keep them from boring each other. People who are in love because they like the same things do not short-circuit their affection, but ground it in the broad fields of all that they look out upon.

No interest so binds a man and woman together

as their children, though nothing could cause them more trouble. The problem of unifying two lives may hardly be accomplished before it is complicated by two or three more. The attention required by the newcomers, the patience and fortitude, would be too much to expect of a couple who married chiefly for other reasons than that of raising babies, were it not that virtues are generated by necessity. The development of character evoked by parental care makes over two relatively irresponsible people into the father and the mother, who, by living anew for their children, acquire the qualities always honored as human and humane.

Beauty belongs to children, because they embody the aspiration of the race. Fresh, helpless, and responsive, they might be very dear even if they were not the repository of all possible value; but it should not diminish their charm to know that their preciousness to the individual may be nature's disguise for their importance to the species. There is no species apart from individuals, and if anything has intrinsic worth it is children, because values are resident in them if anywhere. Certainly

223

children should never be regarded as inferior to their elders. In the procession of generations they have a longer lineage and are older than we; in evolution they are farther along and are younger than we. They have more of a past and more of a future, and would not trade their present for ours.

If the work of an artist in wood or stone is creation, the creation of living beauty is art. Bringing a child into the world is a process no more unreflective than begetting an idea; and bringing a child up in the world can easily employ as much intelligence as developing an inspiration in one of the fine arts. An effective art of caring for babies has been worked out, because people know what they want babies to be. But the older a child grows, the more uncertainty there is about what should be made of him, and the more the responsibility of deciding the question is shirked. Frequently more attention is given to babies than they require, when not enough is given to older children, though a stereotyped procedure must be less satisfactory with differentiated personalities than with infants whose wants can more easily be anticipated. Perhaps it

224

is because babies and youngsters more readily receive affection of the kind which they need, that they are more often lovely than adolescents and adults. Many parents mold a child's life in the beginning as though it were to be a work of art, only to botch the job later.

Several of what formerly were important functions of the family have been taken over by specialized institutions, but the family still has the first and most formative influence on the child. Though industry now is rarely carried on in the home, the chief incentive to it is support of a family, and choice of work is usually determined by the attitude at home. Though government is no longer a family affair, interest in it or indifference to it derives from conversation in the family circle. Religious exercises and teachings have been transferred from home to church, but the hold of church on the child depends largely upon the religious atmosphere in the home. The best school has great difficulty in giving a child an education not appreciated or encouraged by his parents. According to modern psychology, children are so plastic and suggestible that even war may seem natural and instinctive when glorified by parents, intentionally or not.

Living in the presence of his mother and father influences the character of a child more than being born of them. Hence those who share a manifold interest in life are the best parents as well as the happiest lovers. Only people who have made something of themselves through rich experience can be really happy together or make much of their children. From beginning to end the art of love is the art of life.

Chapter Fifteen

THE ART OF EDUCATION

THE art of life is primarily the art of education. Every man wants to live as well as possible, by achieving the values that he thinks important. While he does not like to be unduly interfered with, he is grateful, at least in retrospect, for tips that give him a lift on the way to happiness. When he has discovered short-cuts and sure approaches to the good things of life he would be heartless not to teach them to his children. If he has no children of his own, he still seeks to impart his wisdom to the most receptive minds he can find. As old dogs teach puppies the canine customs, and birds coach fledgelings in avian ways, so do men show their progeny how to be human.

Babies are not born human, and whenever they have been able to grow up without tutelage they have not become human. The psychical and social traits which characterize humanity have to be learned, because the infant is endowed with little but the capacity to receive whatever training his parents and guardians see fit to give him, or give him unwittingly. A man child is more helpless than the offspring of any other animal, but he is the only creature that help can make human. If it is natural for men to teach, it is even more natural for their young to learn. To live they must learn; and they catch on so quickly that soon human conventions seem like instincts to them.

Since they can be taught almost anything, the problem of what to teach them is enormous. Plastic as they are at first, if they learn to be one kind of person they are thereby shut out from being all the other people they might have been. Parents want their children to be different from other children, but not queer. They must have individuality, and they must be able to live in society. They should have all the advantages that can be given them, but they should not be too sheltered to fend for themselves. They should know all that their

228

parents have found worth knowing but no one can tell them what they will have to find out alone. Existence is so complicated and has so many compensating features that conditions which might seem inauspicious for a child often turn out to be favorable. People who try to bring up their children systematically, like the father of George Meredith's Richard Feverel, may blunder conspicuously.

Responsibility cannot be avoided simply by turning children over to professional educators, because without belonging to their profession one cannot be sure which of them are expert. One cannot be on the inside of everything, however. With regard to most specialized knowledge one must be content with straws in the wind that can be watched by the layman. But when parents have chosen as wisely as they can a school for their child, they must remember that after he goes there, as well as before, they may for many years have the chief influence over him. They have a unique opportunity to inspire and guide his interest. The school can do little with him where it lacks the sympathy of his family. What is talked about by the people he normally respects the most is fairly certain to be valued by him, as what is ignored or belittled at home is likely to be disesteemed by him. Later he may get the idea from other people, if it does not occur to him, that it is smart to resent parental solicitude, but in the beginning he is docile.

Once his eyes are opened to the wonder of the big world, it is not hard for his family to interest him in anything toward which they can direct his attention. If they take him for a walk it will be as much fun for him as a ride. If they take him on the street car he will be delighted to ride all the way to the end of the line and back without getting off. Watching the people and the changing scene will absorb him like a circus. If he is kept away from ordinary mortals and their conveyances, he will not feel held back from life, for he will discover as much oddity and variety through the window of a limousine as Dickens could imagine in a tenement. If characters of Greek mythology are often gossiped about at the table, they will become as familiar to him as movie stars could be. If at meals the discussion turns now and then to the relation of hell, purgatory, and heaven in Dante's scheme of things; if the advantages of coal, gas, and oil furnaces are debated as a matter of importance—a child will become as glib about the Dantesque cosmology or the theory of central heating as he could about the rules of football or jacks, the ways to make a sundae or to pitch a baseball.

Nothing is inherently of consequence or without it, but whatever can serve a need has value when we are aware of its usefulness. Things of beauty are the things we live by. We learn to live for them because we cannot live without them. They are food and drink, and our hunger and thirst give them worth. Life is a quest for good things, a preparation of them, consumption of them, and cleaning up after them. Hence meals are the focal points of existence and education. At meal-time are recalled the effort and excitement that preceded, the endeavor and adventure to follow are anticipated, and the refreshment of the present is enjoyed. Values are the bread and the wine of life, and Jesus, who taught men to love life and to have it more abundantly, made the occasion of his final teaching his last supper.

Teaching children to eat symbolizes teaching them to live. The whole world looks good to them in the beginning. Tests show that there is scarcely anything of which they are innately afraid. Babies like to put into their mouths whatever attracts them. Having small experience of their own, and knowing little of what other people have learned, they cannot discriminate values. Anything might be grist for their mill. They not only try to eat sour grapes, but chew up postage stamps, and wall paper when they can get it off. They even swallow dirt. If children later develop distaste for foods that most people like, the explanation may be the example of an older person. Young babies now thrive on vegetables that parents have had great difficulty in feeding to older children, but they are also the nourishment which parents themselves have frequently disliked. Stubbornness is often stimulated in children by an awkward attempt to make them eat what they might have found good if no fuss had been made.

Instruction in the way to eat is as symbolic of general education as lessons in what to eat. Children are being taught to get along in society in being told not to grab, but to ask for things politely; in being cautioned not to ask for what is not on the table; not to make noises; not to hold the knife and fork as if they were 'cello and bow; not to sing at the table; not to talk about certain subjects; and not to interrupt when some one else is talking. No one thing is more important to successful living than learning to eat in a way acceptable to successful people. Without table manners one can hardly be thought "nice" or even intelligent. They are valued so much that without them any beauty is marred. Candidates for the title of Miss America in the Atlantic City beauty contest discover that a faultless shape and a graceful walk are not enough even to put them in the running. They are invited to dinner, that their eating may be observed, before they can hope to represent their home towns, let alone the nation.

233

The finest point in learning the right manners is learning that, despite their importance, they are not all-important; that people who lack them must as far as possible be treated exactly as if they had them. Children should learn that such people may have a different code that is altogether right where they come from. Children should have the experience of eating with all sorts of people to learn that even those whose manners would not be proper anywhere, may be so well educated in some respects that without eating with them one's own education would be neglected.

The younger members of a family usually bring more to the conversation at table than the older ones, and much of what the youngsters report would seem novel to anyone. Seen from their point of view, all their experience is fresh. To take the unworn outlook of their children enables parents to live over again and keep young; while adopting the attitude of their elders gives young people the advantage of age, equipping them with knowledge of the recurrent and permanent features of life, so that they need not be completely surprised by what

234

is in store for them. In meeting about the table the young learn to mature without losing the spontaneity and naïveté which they teach their seniors; while the grown-ups learn from their juniors to keep on growing and wondering without losing the judgment that they pass on. Learning and teaching go best together, and only when people do both are they really living.

Those who live by teaching because they can do nothing else are not good teachers. The good ones are those who cannot help teaching, because they are so successful in whatever they do that they must share the excitement of what they are doing and how they do it. The best teachers of sculpture are sculptors, the best instructors in printing are printers, and the master sculptors and printers are those who continually discover refinements in their art which they must impart to apprentices, who in turn cannot really learn what they are taught until they themselves are able to do it and teach it. Only by working to objectify values can one realize what they are, and when they are realized they reappear in new problems.

For many people learning is the tour of certain things alone considered educational or cultural; and being learned is being able to conduct such a tour without deviating from it. Yet even people of this opinion, when they are not discussing education, often recognize the importance of learning to solve new problems by venturing off the beaten track. They want doctors who are acquainted with the latest ideas in medicine, who have studied with the kind of men who make discoveries, and are themselves in the habit of making them. Wherever intelligence is needed to cope with difficulty, society relies upon persons who have learned to overcome obstacles by doing it.

In pioneer days there was no lack of such people despite the dearth of schools. Boys learned by working with their fathers in the field, and girls by helping their mothers in the house. Now that most men earn their living in such a manner that their sons cannot be with them, and not enough work is done in the home to educate the daughters, the school must teach children the art of life. It was John Dewey's idea that the school could best do this by giving children experience of life's problems, not merely through books, but through watching and practicing the use of tools in various arts. In John Dewey's Laboratory School in Chicago the schedule of girls and boys alike included gardening, sewing, textiles, drawing, modeling, carpentry, cooking, dramatics, and printing.

The children were taken on trips about the city to observe the organization of modern life. Instead of being kept in ignorance or being made ashamed of the fact that their city was hog-butcher to the world, they were conducted through the stockyards from the first squeal to the last smell. They shivered in a cold-storage plant while refrigeration was made plain to them. They saw the markets where vegetables were handled wholesale. They went through a sculptor's studio, where their education was unintentionally advanced when a hastily arranged veil slipped from the shoulders of a model. It would have been in keeping with the spirit of the school to have devised a way to have satisfied more adequately the children's natural curiosity about the human body, and to have ex-

237

plained the mechanism of sex to them when it would have aroused in them the same kind of interest and emotion as the works of a watch or a fire engine. The children visited the city health department to learn how they were protected from disease; and they were entertained in a station of the fire department, where they were allowed to slide down the brass poles. At the steel mills, amid smoke and din, they saw half-naked men pouring molten ore, and moving white-hot bars of metal, in the glare of furnaces that nightly glow against the sky. Night and day they heard the trains, and now and then the ships, that make their city the freight-handler of the nation. Finally they watched the excitement of getting out a newspaper—the racing typewriters, linotype machines, and rotary presses that brought the whole world to the breakfast table where the children saw at least the headlines before they hurried off to school.

The education in John Dewey's school was designed to make the coming generation at home in the life about them, so that outside school and after they had left it, instead of having to put away what they had been taught, they could go on augmenting it. After such a beginning, even were a man to be cloistered later, he would retain some appreciation of the world's work and sympathy for all kinds of workers. His childhood admiration would tinge his respect for all people who do things of benefit to society, and fill him with contempt or pity for persons who could be supercilious toward any labor that serves an honest need.

A man with such an education could hardly be cloistered, no matter how retiring he might be. For him the library and the study would have doors open to life, and every book worth keeping would be of value in living. He would not hesitate to give a large place in education to books, knowing that to neglect them, as college students often do, is to ignore the invention of printing. It is mediæval for a student to rely chiefly on lectures for ideas that he might get first-hand in the library.

Plato said, however, that it was more important to impress thoughts directly on the minds of men than to inscribe them on the pages of books, because books cannot explain when they are misunderstood or questioned, but go on repeating themselves. Teachers who really think before their classes, instead of thumbing over old notes, awaken their students with ideas thought in their presence and for their benefit. The interest in hearing a person talk, which makes the stage interesting, enables many people to profit more from lectures than from books, even when the lectures are ordinary and the books are masterpieces. It is a dramatic performance to address a group of students and hold their attention till the bell rings. Every teacher must recall the qualms he had before facing his first class. If they should not like him they might get up and walk out, or they might stay and make a fool of him. They might jeer him or throw chalk at him or talk together as if he were not there. He would have to make friends with them and keep them on his side. That is half the art of lecturing. The other half is to amuse a class enough to keep from boring them and yet be teaching instead of entertaining them.

Students should gather in large audiences to hear inspirational lectures, and meet with tutors in small groups or privately for guidance and discussion. Students should learn how to study and to plan their time for it before coming to college. It should not be necessary to call the roll in college or to pay any attention to class attendance. A college faculty ought to assume that students come to them to learn, and there should be no objection to absences that do not interfere with learning. At the end of each course students might be granted or refused credit solely on the basis of examination, it being immaterial how they got the content of a course if they have it. Examinations might be given only twice in a student's college career, midway and at the end, or only at the end, covering subjects which presumably could be mastered only by a student who had taken college seriously. A student who could prepare for examination in a shorter time than usual should not be held back to the pace of slower minds.

To graduate or refuse to graduate a student according to the grades and attendance recorded by the registrar's office, regardless of what the student has in his head, is a little quaint. When education is reduced to this, it is inevitable that toward commencement time there should always be pressure brought to bear upon instructors to give to certain people grades that will allow them to graduate, simply because otherwise they would not graduate. If being educated means getting a D in a course instead of an F, when it is within an instructor's power to scratch one mark as easily as another, it seems ruthless to brand anyone as uneducated.

It might be an improvement to abolish all grades but the distinction between those who have got what they are expected to get in college and those who have not. No instructor can indicate with the half-dozen grades at his disposal the shades of differentiation that he can discern in a class. His grading must be arbitrary. He has a vague, ideal standard according to which he may mark a whole class up or down, but usually he is also guided by the actual performance of the students before him, which obliges him to give a B to this one if he gives a C to that one, and so on. Considering their ability, opportunity, and incentive, all students are doing the best they can all the time, and deserve

A's. Considering the same things, they are all doing the worst they can, and should get F's. The ideal would be for people to attend college as long as they are learning something, and to let wisdom, like virtue, be its own reward. But without grades and degrees there would be no neat way of knowing who is educated.

A degree must be judged by the college that confers it, and the college should not be graded too much by its athletic record. There is no more reason why an educational institution should be represented by its athletic teams and rated according to their success than why the stock of a business house should go up and down according to the athletic prowess of its employees. It is right and proper for a circus to be advertised by its athletes and attended for their fame, and people should see spectacles of strength and skill, but colleges should not be called upon to provide them. If colleges must have athletes, however, they should not be obliged to study.

There is much to be said for giving people what they want, and if the purpose of colleges is con-

243

ceived differently now from what it was, they can only continue to function by fostering the values that are demanded of them. Most colleges in this country were denominational in the beginning, their atmosphere was religious, and they trained young men for the ministry. Now college graduates more often go into other professions and business, and college has become largely preparatory for graduate work which is the real preparation for making a living. This is partly the cause and partly the result of the increasing immaturity of college students. They feel self-conscious in calling one another men and women, and find it more natural to say boys and girls, or even kids. Instead of saying that they go to college or the university, they speak of going to school, as if they would prefer to be still in the grades. This may be an unconscious effort to overcome the formality of college, and a good indication that the subject-matter and methods in college are not well related to the character of the students. Education is most successful in kindergarten and the professional school, because there the natural and spontaneous interests of the individual are not at variance with the system. So many college students are unenthusiastic about their studies that even those who are interested often pretend that study is distasteful in order to fit into the atmosphere around them. A distressing number of college students expect to be goaded rather than guided, and are content if they can maneuver to get passing marks without being distracted from "activities" and athletics. Rarely is a professor late to class without their hoping that he will be late enough for them to leave without getting "cuts."

Students apparently do not realize that in institutions which charge for tuition they are paying about eighty cents for each lecture. It might help them to get their money's worth if they had to put down cash each time they entered a classroom. Reluctance to buy books would be absurd, considering their expense compared with that of tuition, were it not that what has been paid all at once in a lump tends to be forgotten, especially when paid by parents, whereas money is twice counted that visibly comes out of one's own pocket. Even in colleges where tuition is free the outlay that most students make to live away from home is out of all proportion to what they are willing to spend on the books that contain what they supposedly went away to learn. Students who live at home during their college course might be reminded that if they are not studious the support they receive from their families is being wasted. It is easy to see why people who work their way through college are most likely to appreciate their studies. Perhaps all students should do something toward earning their own way; and there is much in favor of making it possible for students to be self-supporting, as in the coöperative system where they alternately study and earn money. One need not be a pacifist to see that taking advantage of the penury of students by clothing them and paying them and promising them a rank in case of war, if they will take army training in college, is propaganda. But one need not be a militarist to see that the student armies are making militarism ridiculous.

The merging of the last years in high school with the first years of college may prevent the repetition of preparatory work that too often occurs in the collegiate course. Studies should not be too stiff, but should take for granted that students are maturing, and help them to do so. There is something in the remark of William James that it does not matter what is done in college, because the young grow up somehow during those four years, regardless of what is done. But compared with the mental stature that John Stuart Mill had attained by the time he was twelve, most college graduates are scarcely grown up. Though he began to learn Greek at the age of three, Mill asserts in his *Autobiography* that there was nothing prodigious about his infancy, that any normal child could learn as he did, if tutored as he was. Even if we do not believe this, it may be that the development of many children is retarded because too little is expected of them.

Getting off to a slow start in education is not as bad, however, as dropping intellectual interests after graduation from college. Even those who have got something besides passing grades out of their studies are likely to lose the habit of reading substantial books and of thinking seriously when they lose touch with college. This misfortune is being overcome by adult education in night classes and correspondence work for people who wish to continue their formal education. Some colleges send reading lists to their alumni to help them keep up. The idea is obsolescent that education is merely preparation for life, that learning should stop when living begins. An education is not worth much that is not from the first a part of life; and a life is trifling that does not continue to be educational, in which recurrent, familiar factors are not developed into new dimensions and spiced by continual introduction of variety, as in any work of art. A good education gives a responsive person the chance to fill his mind with thoughts of all that man has achieved or dreamed, and helps him to incorporate in his own life the highest values that he knows.

Chapter Sixteen

THE ART OF LIFE

EDUCATION is never complete, but when it has gone far enough to teach us its shortcoming it has achieved its goal. Because beauty slips away from every art, the best that art can do is to make us aware of values to be sought. Art accomplishes its purpose in pointing beyond itself to beauty unattained, arousing us to the unwon splendor of existence, the inexhaustible freshness of the world. He who could stay awake to this would not need the stimulus of art. He would be an artist—if not with pen or brush, with every act and thought.

To bring order into one's own life is art more surely than giving shape to clay or marble. To learn what one truly wants and to eliminate the rest is to live in the realm of beauty. It is pathetic that people should hate leaving a work of art to go back into everyday life, because they know that impulses now benignly reconciled by art will there conflict, the trivial will swamp the important, and the rhythm will break. As people discriminate ends and seek the means for their achievement, become aware of what they are about, arrange their affairs, economize their efforts and harmonize their thoughts, the smoothness, the power, the enchantment of art will pervade their lives. Then they will be saved from wishing that they were doing something else no matter what they are doing. Having seized upon what is essential, they can jettison the rest. They will have a sense of ease and will breathe freely. Their emotions will flow through deep, unobstructed channels. They will be absorbed in what they do, the excitement of it will carry them on to accomplishment, and the solace of it refresh them for further endeavor. They will not have to tear themselves away from what interests them, no curtain will fall, no guards will turn them out, for this is not a book, a theater, or a museum—it is what life may be.

In making life an art the important thing is for

a man to discover what his ability is, to project his goal in line with it and train himself in that direction. Then he may compact himself to overcome all obstacles, like Cellini, who said on the eve of a competition: "I am so confident in the result of the hard, disciplined study I have devoted to my art, that I think to gain the palm, even were the great Michel Agnolo Buonarroti in the running."[1] When a man has decided what he wants to do, realizing that what he really wants to do he can do, he will reflect like Paul that every man who striveth for the mastery is temperate in all things. He will lay aside everything that hinders him, knowing that there is on every hand a throng of witnesses, and run with perseverance the course that lies before him, because, if athletes carefully train for a perishable crown which only one can win, nothing should distract him from the imperishable crown that all may win.

All may win success in life if they will, simply by choosing and developing their most likely possibilities, after taking stock of themselves as a

[1] Cellini, Benvenuto, *Memoirs*, Everyman edition, p. 451.

painter stands off to look at his picture. Many feel
prevented by bad luck from coming into their own,
but the winners are those who turn even their
limitations to advantage. As Santayana says, "The
intelligent man known to history flourishes within
a dullard and holds a lunatic in leash."[1] Nothing
gives confidence so much as a philosophical faith
like that of Hegel: "As soon as a man recognizes
that what happens to him is merely an evolution
of his self, and that he carries only his own burden,
he holds himself a free agent, and in all that be-
falls him he has the belief that no injustice is done
him."[2]

Nothing stands in the way of a man who does
not stand in his own way. Many people become
discouraged because they want to do something
great in a hurry; but those too impatient to make
something of themselves often spend their time in
self-pity because they are nothing. Balzac said:
"To make plans is to enjoy the fumes of enchanted
cigarettes, but without carrying them out all goes

[1] Santayana, George, *Little Essays*, p. 8.
[2] Hegel, G. W. F., *Logik*, p. 297.

up in revery and smoke."[1] Those who balk at executing desires miss half the fun of living. They should be glad that projects have to be worked out, for, as Shakespeare says, "Things won are done; joy's soul lies in the doing."

Perhaps joy lies not so much in the doing as in consciousness of the power to do. The chief value of achievement may consist in making a man realize his ability. The man aware of power can abide his time, content to remain obscure like Spinoza in a garret, leisurely writing three or four books before he dies. Emily Dickinson did not trouble to publish her thoughts, and Socrates and Jesus never wrote theirs down. Power is usually quiet and deliberate. It accumulates in a patient man like Henry Ford and evaporates from one in a fever to set the Thames afire.

The successful man is persistent when results are long postponed. To remember that things well begun are half done may not be sufficient encouragement, but it is reassuring to believe with Hegel that in a real sense the end is present in the begin-

[1] Quoted by Sainte-Beuve, C. A., in *Causeries du Lundi*, ii, p. 353.

ning: "Unsatisfied striving disappears when we realize that the final object of the world is even now fulfilled, since it eternally fulfills itself."[1] To think of performing an act is more than the first step, because the whole act is present in the thought. To do anything significant a plan of action is necessary. One cannot write a book without something to say, and what Michelangelo said of painting may be said of all successful living—it is done with the head more than with the hands.

Ideas often come from handling things, however, and men have rightly so much confidence in experimental manipulation that they like to go through motions to convince themselves that they are not dreaming. Not only children and simple souls are impressed by observable industry with its noise and commotion. The professor is fascinated by the activity of men wielding picks and shovels, backing and dumping trucks and guiding steam rollers, because these men seem plainly to be accomplishing something. His own achievements are so difficult to gauge that he himself often

[1] Hegel, G. W. F., *Logik*, p. 407.

doubts their importance. Seated with a book, he may hear the whir of an airplane, look out the window to see it streaking across the sky, and think to himself that there is a chap who is getting somewhere. But if he is reading Santayana he may come across the remark that the aviator is merely a new kind of sailor, that the only sublimity of which man is capable is intellectual. The flier is not closer to heaven for being up in the air, and his speed is probably not hastening his approach to happiness. The only thing that can get a man anywhere, or make it worth while to be going anywhere, is the art of life. Travel is a fool's paradise unless one knows how to live, and he who knows how to live does not need to travel, since he can live happily at home. Yet he best can enjoy travel because he is everywhere at home.

Most men prefer movement to meditation; they are men of action who see no activity in thought, though only as they think about it can they find value in what they do. Chafing to act, they do not see that there is more action in the soliloquies of Hamlet than in the murders of Macbeth. Philosophers have said that God's life is pure act because it is pure thought, and that only a thoughtful life is worthy of man. To act thoughtlessly is to be acted upon by circumstances, like an unintelligent animal or inanimate object. Only by taking thought can man direct his life toward worthwhile ends.

A man of force is not worried to see his goal a long way off, knowing that a goal should properly be distant. He does not seek diversion like those who wish to forget their laziness or weakness. Nor is he afraid of fun like those who are too tense in the effort to get ahead. Like Leonardo or Michelson he knows that inspiration often comes in leisure, and does not make futile motions at his work when tired. He knows not only that his work will be better for his play, but that no work should prevent his being human. Santayana says: "It is not wisdom to be only wise."[1] And Spinoza: "I say it is the part of a wise man to refresh and recreate himself with moderate and pleasant food and drink, and also with perfumes, with the soft beauty of growing plants, with dress, with music, with

[1] Santayana, George, *Sonnet III.*

many sports, with theatres, and the like, such as every man may make use of without injury to his neighbor."[1]

It is important not to injure one's neighbor, because the art of life consists largely in getting along with other people. Man can carry on very few of his characteristic activities without social support or approval. To some extent he can ignore the opinion of other people and not care whom he affronts, but even the powerful individual finds it easier and more graceful to ingratiate himself with others than to needlessly offend them. It is not only human to be considerate and sympathetic— it is intelligent, which also is human. In fact, sympathy has little depth or range without being intelligent; and genuine intelligence in the art of life is sympathetic, since life must be lived with other people, and since man cannot be happy without family and friends and social interests.

A man who has no kindness in him, or who for other reasons cannot coöperate with his fellows, must be ostracized or incarcerated. Many a martyr

---

[1] Spinoza, Baruch, *The Ethics*, part iv, prop. xlv, note.

might have been tolerated or honored in another time and place; but a man must be tactful enough to get along to some extent with the people around him in order to be known and claimed by kindred spirits elsewhere. Socrates was seventy years old before he was asked to drink the hemlock, and he accepted his sentence as just, inasmuch as he had become intolerable to the state on which depended the kind of life he wished to live. If we agree with Plato that Socrates was the wisest and justest of men, we seem to have a case in which intelligence and sympathy were disastrous. But Socrates saw that his real life, that of teaching the art of life, would be likely to survive his death only if he did to the end what he had taught to be wise and just.

On account of his kindly wisdom we cannot think of Socrates as criminal, and no man is criminal in so far as he is intelligent and sympathetic, but only in so far as he is ignorant and callous. Warner Fite says: "For my own part, I seem to find ever less use for such terms as 'wicked,' 'sinful,' 'nefarious,' and the like. They seem to me to correspond to nothing real. And I tend rather to think of those who are morally inadmissible as 'coarse,' 'brutal,' or 'insensitive.' "[1] A good man is one who is sensitive to the welfare of others, and who thinks about it. Ability to survey the social results of behavior depends upon awareness of the point of view of other people. One cannot be considerate where one is ignorant. Hence intelligence is essential to true sympathy, and *vice versa.* "As the only effective thought is one fused by emotion into a dominant interest, so the only truly general, the reasonable as distinct from the merely shrewd or clever thought, is the generous thought."[2]

Man's capacity to criticize his conduct, to shape it by and large, and make plans with reference to an inclusive, social end, is his most human and valuable trait, the one that should be cultivated above all if his life is to be an art. Living his own life in relation to the life about him is not only a man's duty to others, but to himself, because the only self worth having is one that is interested in many things beyond itself. John Stuart Mill says:

[1] Fite, Warner, *Moral Philosophy*, p. 189.
[2] Dewey, John, and Tufts, J. H., *Ethics*, p. 334.

259

"When people who are tolerably fortunate in their outward lot do not find in life sufficient enjoyment to make it valuable to them, the cause generally is, caring for nobody but themselves. To those who have neither public nor private affections, the excitements of life are much curtailed. . . . A cultivated mind . . . finds sources of inexhaustible interest in all that surrounds it; in the objects of nature, the achievements of art, the imaginations of poetry, the incidents of history, the ways of mankind, past and present, and their prospects in the future."[1] A man whose self is opened up to remote meanings, which constantly flow into it, will never lack immediate interests, or ever despise what is at hand, because he will see that every experience has infinite significance. He will say with Santayana: "The happy filling of a single hour is so much gained for the universe at large, and to find joy and sufficiency in the flying moment is perhaps the only means open to us for increasing the glory of eternity"[2]

[1] Mill, John Stuart, *Utilitarianism*, chap. ii.
[2] Santayana, George, *Little Essays*, p. 104.

Activity is not only directed toward ends, but has value in itself, if it is anything for a man to be doing. Whatever lacks this double significance should be shunned. Perhaps nothing could be found which neither had any interest nor led to anything of interest. But some things are relatively more important than others, and nothing is worth while unless human interest makes it a repository of meaning and associates it with other meanings. When a man becomes attached to a dog the virtues of all other dogs focus in his pet. At the same time the dog awakens his master's interest in other dogs, so that he notices them and recognizes their importance where he might otherwise have ignored them. When a man marries, his wife becomes all women to him, and in all women he sees something of his wife. When a man reads a book, all that he has ever read comes in to light up its pages, and it in turn will help to illuminate other books. This centripetal and centrifugal movement of the attention brings the universe to every point of interest, and radiates from every interesting point to the ends of the earth.

261

All the arts foster the human tendency to stress what unity there is in the variety of experience, and to invent security on the surface of the unknown. They help man to hope that life itself can be a work of art in which there is no real ugliness because everything contributes to the beauty of the whole. It is not hard for those who feel fortune's arm about the waist to be buoyant and trusting, to see romance in dirt that does not touch their skirts, color in crime that does not soil their souls, nobility in suffering that does not smother their hopes, quaintness in tenements that do not stifle their children, beautiful sunsets in fumes that do not poison their atmosphere, drama in tragedy that does not blast their lives. But when fortune slips away from her darlings, even in imagination, a flood of ugliness rises to their lips. Then they cry out with Vachel Lindsay, not that they die, but that they die like sheep. The arts that comfort us, how can they comfort the unfortunate? And if they cannot comfort them, what is their comfort to us?

Yet the most inspiring artists have usually sprung from unfortunate circumstances. Though great artists have come from favored homes, all artists are people aware of the insecurity of life. To them distinctions in the human lot are trifling after seeing that all men are afloat on the same earth, going they know not whither, and unable to steer. Because artists realize the human predicament, they earnestly seek a solution, and find it in developing what control of life on earth is possible through art.

To think of life and art as opposed categories impoverishes both. Art can have little significance unless it represents values in the problems of life; while life can have little meaning unless its problems are clarified and its ideals objectified by art. Life is the content of art, and art is the form of life. All the arts are part of the art of life. Like philosophy and religion, business, science, and education, they are all designed to make life endurable and death bearable. Architecture surrounds and overarches men, to make them feel at home and forget that they do not know where they are. Music brings harmony into human lives, painting composes them, sculpture balances them, dancing

263

poises them; the movies, literature, printing, and the theater amuse or instruct them; and love comforts them.

Because life is desperate there is hope in art. Because life is ugly there is belief in beauty. Art is life aspiring to beauty through human ingenuity and effort. Life does not always achieve the values which are contemplated in beauty; art does not always surmount the difficulties that give it birth. Success shines against a background of failure, but, despite all discouragement, as long as there is life there is art.

THE END

Bibliography

ÆSTHETIC THEORY

BUERMEYER, LAURENCE, *The Aesthetic Experience.*

CROCE, BENEDETTO, *Aesthetics; Breviary of Aesthetics.*

DUCASSE, CURT JOHN, *Philosophy of Art.*

EDMAN, IRWIN, *The World, the Arts, and the Artist.*

GORDON, KATE, *Esthetics.*

HARTMAN, HENRY G., *Aesthetics.*

LANGFELD, H. S., *The Aesthetic Attitude.*

LEE, VERNON, *The Beautiful.*

MEAD, GEORGE H., "The Nature of the Aesthetic Experience," in the *International Journal of Ethics,* Vol. XXXVI, No. 4, July, 1926.

PARKER, DEWITT H., *The Principles of Aesthetics; The Analysis of Art.*

PARKHURST, HELEN HUSS, *Beauty.*

PRALL, D. W., *Aesthetic Judgment.*

PUFFER, ETHEL, *The Psychology of Beauty.*

RANDALL, JOHN HERMAN, *Our Changing Civilization,* Ch. XI.

SANTAYANA, GEORGE, *The Sense of Beauty; Reason in Art.*

TOLSTOY, LYOF N., *What Is Art?*

BIBLIOGRAPHY

TUFTS, J. H., "Beauty" and "Aesthetics" in Baldwin's
Philosophical Dictionary.

THE MOVIES

BALL, EUSTACE HALE, *The Art of the Photoplay.*
LINDSAY, VACHEL, *The Art of the Moving Picture.*

THE THEATER

CHANDLER, FRANK W., *Aspects of Modern Drama.*
CRAIG, GORDON, *On the Art of the Theatre.*
MACGOWAN, KENNETH, *The Theatre of Tomorrow.*

PAINTING AND SCULPTURE

ABBOT, EDITH R., *The Great Painters.*
BARNES, ALBERT C., *The Art in Painting.*
CHENEY, SHELDON, *A Primer of Modern Art.*
GARDNER, HELEN, *Art Through the Ages.*
MULLEN, MARY, *An Approach to Art.*
RODIN, AUGUSTE, *Art.*
RUSKIN, JOHN, *Modern Painters.*
STURGIS, RUSSELL, *Appreciation of Sculpture.*

MUSIC

BEKKER, PAUL, *The Story of Music.*
DISERENS, CHARLES M., *The Influence of Music on Behavior.*

266

BIBLIOGRAPHY

GRAY, CECIL, *The History of Music.*
SULLIVAN, J. W. N., *Beethoven.*

DANCING

DUNCAN, ISADORA, *My Life.*
JACQUES-DALCROZE, EMILE, *Rhythm, Music, and Education.*
KINNEY, TROY and MARGARET WEST, *The Dance.*

ARCHITECTURE

ADAMS, HENRY, *Mont-Saint-Michel and Chartres.*
CHENEY, SHELDON, *The New World Architecture.*
RUSKIN, JOHN, *Seven Lamps of Architecture.*

LITERATURE

AMES, VAN METER, *Aesthetics of the Novel.*
BROWN, ROLLO WALTER, *The Writer's Art.*
EASTMAN, MAX, *The Enjoyment of Poetry.*
FRANCE, ANATOLE, *On Life and Letters.*
MACHEN, ARTHUR, *The Hill of Dreams.*
MURRY, J. MIDDLETON, *Discoveries; The Problem of Style.*
SCHOPENHAUER, ARTHUR, *The Art of Literature.*
STEVENSON, ROBERT LOUIS, *Essays; Letters.*

267

BIBLIOGRAPHY

Printing

Orcutt, William Dana, *The Kingdom of Books; Master Makers of the Book.*

Business and Science as Art

Beard, Charles A., *Whither Mankind.*
Dewey, John, *The Quest for Certainty.*
Eddington, A. S., *The Nature of the Physical World.*
Tufts, J. H., *The Real Business of Living.*
Whitehead, A. N., *Science and the Modern World.*

Philosophy and Religion as Art

Ames, Edward Scribner, *Religion; The Psychology of Religious Experience; The New Orthodoxy; The Higher Individualism; The Divinity of Christ.*
Durant, Will, *The Story of Philosophy.*
Potter, Charles Francis, *The Story of Religion.*
Santayana, George, *Poetry and Religion; Three Philosophical Poets.*
Wright, W. K., *A Student's Philosophy of Religion.*

The Art of Love

Keyserling, Hermann, *The Book of Marriage.*
Lombroso, Gina, *The Soul of Woman.*
Stopes, Marie, *Married Love.*
Van de Velde, Th. H., *The Perfect Marriage.*

268

BIBLIOGRAPHY

THE ART OF EDUCATION

DEWEY, JOHN, *The School and Society.*
DIMNET, ERNEST, *The Art of Thinking.*
MILL, JOHN STUART, *Autobiography.*
RUSSELL, BERTRAND, *Education and the Good Life.*
WALLAS, GRAHAM, *The Art of Thought.*

THE ART OF LIFE

DEWEY, JOHN, *Human Nature and Conduct.*
ELLIS, HAVELOCK, *The Dance of Life.*
RUSSELL, BERTRAND, *The Conquest of Happiness.*
SANTAYANA, GEORGE, *The Life of Reason.*

General Index

271

GENERAL INDEX

tive, 2; and taste, xii; ubiquitous, 6-7, 28, 34, 187; in
ugliness, 80; value of, xii, 3
Beethoven, L. von, 100
Bernhardt, Sarah, 63-65
Bodoni, Giambattista, 158
Books, expensive and cheap,
157; and lectures, 240; and
literature, 144-145; in movies,
46-47; reluctance to buy, 245-
246; values in, 144-145
Business, as art, 182-183; like
religion, 185; allied to science,
184

Cathedral, 128-130
Children, beauty of, 9, 223;
docility of, 230; interest in
life, 230; plasticity of, 228;
parental influence on, 225;
and reading, 166; teaching,
227-228; value of, 223-224;
as work of art, 224-225
Choreography, 109
Christ. See Jesus
Church, and fine arts, 206; and
theater, 56
City, beauty of, 130; future, 132-
134; planning, 130-131
Civilization, of Egypt, Greece,
Rome, Twentieth Century, 121
College, degree, 243; examinations, 241; expense of, 245-
246; grades, 241-243; immaturity of students, 244;
methods in, 244-245; religious
atmosphere of, 244
Columbus, Christopher, 167
Cynics, 189
Cyrenaics, 188

Dancing, bodily discipline, 111-
112; and Christianity, 114-
115; defined, 106; and the
Greeks, 114; and nature, 108;
new compared with old, 109-
110; and other arts, 107; and
primitive men, 114; relation
to religion, 115; rhythm of,
115-116; structure of, 109;
symbolism of, 116-117;
technique of, 109; values in,
106
Da Vinci. See Leonardo
Design, in dancing, 109; with
marionettes, 60; with people,
71; of steamships, 21
Desires. See Wishes
Didot, Firmin, 157
Doves Bindery, 158
Dreams. See Wishes
Duncan, Isadora, 108-109

Education, of adults, 247-248;
expense of, 245-246; and
life, 248; in sex, 237-238;
most successful, 244; in solving problems, 236; and the
table, 230-235
El Greco, 195
Empathy, 113-114
Epicureans, 189, 208

Faith, of common people, 199;
of philosopher, 199
Fine arts, and church, 206;
broadly defined, xii; arbitrary
limitation of, 16, 28-29; relation to reality, 39; and useful
arts, 15-16
Furniture, 126

Index of Authors and Titles

277

INDEX OF AUTHORS AND TITLES

278

INDEX OF AUTHORS AND TITLES